WHY I KILLED GANDHI

NATHURAM GODSE

LAUNCHPAD

An imprint of
Srishti Publishers & Distributors

Srishti Publishers & Distributors
A unit of AJR Publishing LLP
212A, Peacock Lane
Shahpur Jat, New Delhi - 110 049

editorial@srishtipublishers.com

First published by Launchpad,
An imprint of Srishti Publishers & Distributors in 2024

10 9 8 7 6 5 4 3 2 1

Printed and bound in India

CONTENTS

THE INCIDENTS AND INVESTIGATION

On 20th January 1948, Mahatma Gandhi was putting up at the Birla House, New Delhi. It was his usual practice to offer prayers in the evening. Members of the Public were free to attend his prayers. There is a platform behind the Birla House, where prayers used to be offered.

On 20th January 1948, at about 5 p.m., Mahatma Gandhi, as usual, proceeded to the prayer platform and began offering prayers. At about 5:15 p.m. an explosion took place at a distance of about 150 yards from where he was offering prayers. A number of persons rushed in the direction where the explosion had taken place. A young man was seen standing some distance away from the scene of the explosion. The persons standing there were saying that he was the individual who had placed a 'bomb' there and had applied a match-stick to it. He was caught hold of then and there, and marched off to the main gate of the Birla house, and handed over to the Police.

This person is said to be Madanlal K. Pahwa, accused No. 4. On a search being made of his person, a live hand-grenade was recovered from the right-hand inside pocket of his coat. The F.I.R. in the case was lodged by Mr. K. N. Sahaney, Magistrate, 1st class, Karnal, who happened to be present in the prayer meeting and had rushed to the scene of the explosion.

The F.I.R. was taken down under sections 4 and 5 of the Explosive Substances Act.

On 30th January 1948, at about 5:00 p.m. Mahatma Gandhi, as usual, proceeded to the prayer-platform. He was accompanied by a number of persons. A large crowd was awaiting his arrival at the prayer platform. Mahatma Gandi climbed up the stairs of the prayer platform. When he had gone 6-7 paces, the crowd opened up into a lane to enable him to pass through.

A person came out of the crowd into the lane in front of Mahatma Gandhi and fired three shots at point-blank range in quick succession at him with a pistol. He was caught hold of then and there. This person is said to be Nathuram V. Godse, accused No. 1. Mahatma Gandhi fell down uttering the words 'Hei Ram'. He was picked up and taken to his room in the Birla House. He, however, succumbed to the injuries sustained by him soon after he had been taken to his room. The F.I.R. in the case was lodged by Mr Nandlal Mehta, who happened to be present at the time at the prayer platform. The F.I.R. was taken down under section 302 of the I.P.C.

The investigation in regard to the explosion incident was begun by the Delhi Police on 20th January 1948. The investigation in regard to the murder incident was begun by the Delhi Police on 30th January 1948.

On 31st January 1948, Mr. J. D. Nagarvala, Deputy Commissioner of Police, Bombay City, was appointed as Superintendent of Police, Delhi, in addition to his own duties, and the investigations in regard to the explosion incident and the murder incident were then taken up by him.

Digambar R. Badge (now approver) was arrested at Poona on 31st January; Dattatraya S. Parchure (accused No. 8) was kept as a detenue at Gwalior with effect from 3rd February 1948, and was shown as under arrest in the case with effect from 17th February. Gopal V. Godse (accused No. 6) was arrested at Uksan (Poona} on 5th February. Vinayak D. Savarkar (accused No. 7) was kept as a detenue with effect from 5th February, and was shown as under arrest in the case with effect from 11th February. Shankar Kistayya (accused No. 5) was arrested at Bombay on 6th February. Narayan D. Apte and Vishnu R. Karkare (accused Nos. 2 and 3) were arrested at Bombay on 14th February.

On 11th February, Shankar Kistayya led two panches along with a police-party to a place just behind the Hindu Mahasabha Bhawan, New Delhi, and took out from one place a live hand-grenade, a gun-cotton-slab with fuse wire and 25 cartridges; from another place 2 live hand-grenades. They were lying buried there.

On 18th February, Dattatraya S. Parchure made a confession before Mr. R.B. Atal, Magistrate 1st Class, Lashkar (Gwalior).

On 26th February, Narayan D. Apte took two panches along with a police party to a place behind the Hindu Mahasabha Bhawan, where he said they had tried out a pistol. A tree with four bullet-marks was shown by him. The branches of the tree containing the bullet-marks were cut and taken possession of. Narayan D. Apte also pointed out a place from where he said the pistol had been fired. An empty cartridge case was found lying there, and was taken possession of.

On 27th February, Narayan D. Apte took two panches along with a police party to the house of Dattatraya S. Parchure at Gwalior. He led them to the back courtyard and pointed out a place where he said Nathuram V. Godse had tried out a pistol.

A number of bullet-marks were found on the wall. A spent-bullet was found lying there, and was taken possession of.

The Police submitted the charge-sheet on 27th February 1948 against Nathuram V. Godse, Narayan D. Apte, Vishnu R. Karkare, Digambar R. Badge (approver), Madanlal K. Pahwa, Shankar Kistayya, Gopal V. Godse, Vinayak D. Savarkar and Dattatraya S. Parchure, u/ss 120-B, 109, 114 and 115 of the I.P.C., read with Section 302 of the I.P.C., u/ss 3, 4, 5 and 6 of the Explosive Substances Act, and u/s 19 of the Indian Arms Act.

THE EVENTS

It was the Court of the Special Judge, Red Fort, Delhi. The prosecution had concluded its evidence in the Mahatma Gandhi Murder Case, viz, Rex versus Nathuram Vinayak Godse and others.

The Special Judge, Shri Atma Charan, had taken his seat. Quiet enveloped the Courtroom. The accused were seated in their respective seats in the dock. Counsels on either side were present. The Press reporters were ready tensely holding their pens.

The Courtroom was packed to capacity. People were allowed entry only with passes.

The say of the accused was going to be heard. The day was 8th November 1948.

The Judge started examination of the accused under Section 342 of the Criminal Procedure Code. He announced:

"Accused No. 1 Nathuram Vinayak Godse, Hindu, age 37 years, Editor, Hindu Rashtra Poona."

Nathuram was up on his legs immediately after hearing 'Accused No. 1'.

"You have heard," the Judge continued, "the entire evidence produced on behalf of the prosecution as against you. What have you to say with regard to it?"

"I am to submit my written statement, Your Honor," Nathuram replied.

"Go ahead, read your statement," said the Judge. At this stage Shri Daphtari, the Advocate General stood up to object.

He said, "Your Honor, the accused may be allowed to depose only what is consistent with this case. Otherwise, he may not be allowed to read his statement."

The Judge disallowed the objection.

Nathuram stood poised before the microphone to read from his written statement. The silence which had hollowed the Courtroom was accentuated by the relay of echoes from the walls with his clear and resonant words.

NATHURAM GODSE'S ANSWER TO THE CHARGE SHEET

I, Nathuram Vinayak Godse, the first accused above named respectfully beg to state as under:

1. Before I make my submission as regards the various charges, I respectfully submit that the charges as framed are not according to law, in as much as there is a misjoinder of charges and there ought to have been two separate trials to the incident of the 20th of January 1948 and the other relating to the incident of the 30th of January 1948. The two having been mixed up together, the whole trial is vitiated.
2. Without prejudice to my above submission I make my submission in respect of the various charges as framed as stated hereafter.
3. In the charge-sheet preferred against the accused, a number of counts have been stated and each of the accused individually and jointly with others has been charged with the commission of the various offences punishable under the Indian Penal Code and other statutes.
4. It appears from the charge sheet that the prosecution takes the events that have happened on 20th January 1948 and thereafter on 30th January 1948 as one and the same or a chain of events in continuation of one and the same object culminating in the murder of Gandhiji.

I therefore, wish to make it clear at the outset that the events up to 20th January 1948 are quite independent and they have no connection whatsoever with what happened thereafter and on 30th January 1948.

5. The first and the foremost amongst the said charges is the charge of conspiracy amongst the accused to murder Gandhiji. I shall therefore first, deal with the same. I say that there was no, conspiracy of any kind whatsoever amongst the accused to commit any of the offences mentioned in the charge-sheet. I may also state here that I have not been abetted by any of the other accused in the commission of the alleged offences.

6. I say that the evidence led by the Prosecution in this regard does not establish and prove that there was any conspiracy whatsoever.

   The only witness who deposes about the alleged conspiracy is Digambar R. Badge (Prosecution Witness 57). He is a totally unreliable witness as will be shown to Your Honor by my counsel when he will explain the evidence in the case and deal with the evidence of this witness, P.W. 57.

7. As regards the charge of collecting and transporting arms and ammunition without license, and abetment thereof on 20th January 1948, I say that I deny the said charge and say that I neither carried or transported gun-cotton slabs, hand-grenades, detonators, wicks, pistols, or revolvers and cartridges etc. as alleged, nor did I have under my control any of such arms and/or ammunition, nor did I

abet and aid any of the accused to do so either before or on or about the 20th January 1948 or any other date. I deny therefore that I contravened any of the provisions of the Indian Arms Act or the Indian Explosives Substances Act and that I committed any offence punishable under the said Acts.

8. The main evidence in regard to this charge is 'the evidence of Digambar R. Badge (P.W. 57), but as stated in paragraph 6 above, he is a totally unreliable witness. This witness Badge (P.W. 57) is known to me but he hardly used to come to me nor have I ever visited his place of residence since several years past. His statement that he came to the Hindu Rashtra office on 10th January 1948, being brought there by Apte ... the accused No. 2 ... is totally false and I deny that the said Badge saw me at the Hindu Rashtra office or any other place on that day, or that in my presence Apte and he had any talk amongst themselves about gun-cotton slabs, hand grenades, etc. and about the delivery thereof at Bombay as falsely alleged by the said Badge. His statement that Apte asked me to come out of the room and that Apte told me that Badge was prepared to hand over the hand grenades etc. and that once work was over is totally false. This is a story got up by Badge to implicate me and others into the alleged conspiracy. I further say that I neither saw nor met Badge on 14th January 1948 at Dadar either alone or in the company of Apte. I did not even know that Badge had come to Bombay on that day.

9. I further deny that I had in my possession or under my control, while at Delhi or abetted any one to have and possess on 20th January 1948, any arms or ammunition as stated in the charge-sheet under the heading "Secondly" paragraphs B (1) and (2). Here also the evidence to support this charge is of Badge alone and I say that he has given false evidence to save his own skin; for on that condition alone he could secure the pardon promised and granted to him.
10. As regards the charge under the heading "Thirdly", I say that I deny the said charge and the abetment thereof as stated in several paragraphs A (1) and (2), and B (1) and (2).
11. As regards the charge under the heading "Fourthly" paragraph 2, I deny that I abetted Madanlal K Pahwa either myself alone or along with others to explode a gun-cotton slab on 20th January 1948 at Birla House. I say that there is no evidence to substantiate this charge and whatever little evidence there may be, can hardly connect me with the explosion of the gun-cotton slab.
12. As regards the charge of abetment in the "attempt to commit the murder of Mahatma Gandhi" under the said heading "Fifthly" in the charge sheet, I deny the said charge and say I had no connection either directly or indirectly with Madanlal K. Pahwa or any other person whatsoever. I say there is no evidence whatsoever to support this charge.
13. As regards the charge under the heading "Sixthly" in the

charge-sheet as to paragraphs (A) (1) and (2) thereof, I say that I have not imported or bought unlicensed pistol and ammunition with the assistance of Narayan D. Apte. I also deny that Dr. Dattatraya S. Parchure and Narayan D. Apte procured the said pistol, or any one of them individually or jointly; abetted me or themselves each other in such procurement of the said pistol and the ammunition. I further say that the evidence produced by Prosecution in that behalf is not reliable. Without prejudice to the above, I further say that even if the acts mentioned in these paragraphs A (1) and (2) may have been committed; this Honorable Court has no jurisdiction to take any notice of them. I further say that so far as I am concerned, the charge, if any, would merge under the charge in paragraph B (1) under this head.

14. As regards the charge under paragraph B (1) and (2) I admit that I had in my possession an automatic pistol No. 606824 and cartridges. But I say that neither Narayan D. Apte nor Vishnu R. Karkare had anything to do with the pistol in my possession.

15. But before I pass to the charge under the heading "Seventhly", it will not be out of place to explain here how I happened to come to Delhi, and why I came to Delhi. I had never made a secret about the fact that I supported the ideology or the school which was opposed to that of Gandhiji. I firmly believed that the teachings of absolute Ahimsa' as advocated by Gandhiji would ultimately result in the emasculation of the Hindu community and thus

make the community incapable of resisting the aggression or inroads of other communities especially the Muslims. To counteract this evil, I resolved to enter public life and formed a group of persons who held like views. In this Apte and I took a leading part and as a part of propaganda started a daily newspaper Agrani. I might mention here that it was not so much the Gandhian 'Ahimsa' teachings that were opposed to by me and my group, but Gandhiji while advocating his views always showed or evinced a bias for Muslims, prejudicial and detrimental to the Hindu community and its interests. I have fully described my point of view hereafter in detail and have quoted numerous instances which unmistakably establish how Gandhiji became responsible for a number of calamities which the Hindu community had to undergo and suffer.

16. In my papers 'Agrani' and 'Hindu Rashtra', I always strongly criticized Gandhiji's views and his methods such as fast for achieving his object, and after Gandhiji started holding prayer meetings, we, Apte and myself - decided to stage peaceful demonstrations showing opposition. We had made such demonstrations at Panchagani, Poona, Bombay and Delhi. There was a wide gulf between the two ideologies and it became wider and wider as concessions after concessions were being made to the Muslims, either at the suggestion or connivance of Gandhiji and the Congress which was guided by Gandhiji, culminating in the partition of the Country on 15th of August 1947. I have dealt with this point in detail hereafter. On 13th of January 1948, I learnt that

Gandhiji had decided to go on fast unto death. The reason given for such fast was that he wanted an assurance of Hindu-Muslim unity in Indian Dominion. But I and many others could easily see that the real motive behind the fast was not merely the so-called Hindu-Muslim Unity, but to compel the Dominion Government to pay the sum of Rs. 55 crores to Pakistan, the payment of which was emphatically refused by the Government. As an answer to this, Apte suggested the same old method to stage a strong but peaceful demonstration at the prayer meetings of Gandhiji. I consented to this half-heartedly, because I could easily see its futility. However, I agreed to join him as no alternative plan was as yet fixed in my mind.

It was for this reason that N.D. Apte and myself went to Bombay on the 14th of January, 1948.

17. On 15th of January, 1948 we – Apte and I – happened to go to the Hindu Sabha Office at Dadar in the morning. I happened to see Badge there. On seeing N.D. Apte and I, Badge talked to N.D. Apte and asked him the reason of his coming to Bombay. Apte told him the reason. Badge thereupon, of his own accord offered to come, to Delhi and join in the demonstration, if we had no objection to his coming there. We wanted men to back us and to shout slogans and we therefore accepted his offer. We told him as to when we were starting.

Badge thereupon told Apte that he had to give some stuff to Pravinchandra Sethia, that he would do so in a day or two and see us on the 17th January 1948.

18. After we met Badge on the 15th of January, 1948 in the Hindu Sabha Office at Dadar, I saw Badge on the 17th of January, 1948 in the morning.
19. The statements made by Badge about our going to Dixitji Maharaj along with him and seeing Dixitji Maharaj, about Apte having told Badge that Savarkar had entrusted Apte and myself the task of finishing Gandhiji, Pandit Jawaharlal and Suhrawardy is a pure concoction and product of Badge's brain. Neither Apte nor I have said anything like this to Badge or any other person. I deny categorically what the Prosecution has so falsely maintained that I was guided in my action by Veer Savarkar and that, but for his complicity, I could never have acted in the way I have done. I take the strongest exception to this untrue and unjust charge and I further regard it as an insult to my intelligence and judgment. The Prosecution's attempt to make out that I was a mere tool in someone else's hands is an aspersion which is far from the truth. Indeed it is a perversion of it.
20. Badge's statements to the effect that I also wanted to go to Poona to meet my brother Gopal Godse who had undertaken to make arrangements for procuring a revolver and to bring him down to Bombay for accompanying us to Delhi, is also untrue. I had no talk with Badge when I met him on the 15th January 1948 except what is stated in paragraph 17 above. Further the statement of Badge that he met me on 16th January 1948 at Poona is also false. The alleged report of my conversation with him at Poona

as deposed to by Badge, in his evidence is also false and untrue. I was not in Poona on 16th January 1948. It will be clear from this that it is not true that I gave him any pistol on that day for being exchanged for a big revolver.

21. I have already stated that we – Apte and myself – had planned to stage a strong but peaceful demonstration at Gandhiji's prayer meeting at the earliest possible opportunity at Delhi, and for the purpose Apte and I were to go there. As stated in paragraph 17, Badge offered to come to Delhi to take part in the demonstration referred to above. We felt an urgent need of taking some volunteers with us for a successful demonstration. Before we started for Delhi we started collecting money to meet the expenses for the journey and for the expenses of the volunteers.

22. I emphatically deny that we saw Savarkar on the 17 January 1948 or that Savarkar blessed us with the words 'Yashasvi Houn Ya,' Be successful and come; Similarly, I also deny that we had any conversation with Badge or that Apte or myself uttered the words-

"Tatyaravani ase Bhavishya kele ahe ki Gandhijichi shambhar varshe

bharali-ata apale kam nishchita honar yat kahi sanshaya nahi;-"

After we met Badge on the 15th of January, 1948 at the Hindu Sabha Office at Dadar, we – Apte and myself – went on our business in connection with the Press.

23. Apte and I came to Delhi by plane on the 17th January 1948 and we put up at the Marina Hotel. On the morning of the 20th of January, 1948 Badge came to the hotel and informed Apte in my presence that he and his servant Kistaiyya would go to the prayer ground in the evening with Apte just to see the scene of prayer where demonstrations would be held. When Badge came in the morning I was lying down on bed as I was feeling unwell owing to severe headache and I told Badge that I may not go to the prayer-ground as I was unwell. The statements of Badge that Apte, Gopal Godse, Karkare, Madanlal, Badge and his servant Madanlal all collected at Marina Hotel, that Madanlal and Badge had their meals there, that Gopal Godse was found repairing the revolver, that Apte, Karkare, Madanlal and Badge went to the Bath-room and were fixing the detonators, Fuse-wires and primers to the gun-cotton stabs and hand-grenades or that Madanlal and I were standing at the either side of the door of the room are entirely false. Badge has put in my mouth the words "Badge, this is our last effort; the work must be accomplished... see to it that everything is arranged properly."

I deny that I addressed the said or similar words to Badge on that day or any other day. As stated before, Badge came to the room in the morning and informed me that he would attend the prayer-meeting in the evening. We had no meeting at all on that day in my room as stated by Badge. Gopal Godse, to my knowledge, was not even in Delhi.

Nobody arranged or fixed detonators fuse-wires or primers to gun-cotton slabs or hand-grenades in the room. In fact, there was no such ammunition either with me or with Apte. Badge's vivid description about the distribution of arms and ammunition amongst the party and about assumption of false names is all false. It is not necessary for me to discuss the evidence and show the falsity of these statements as my counsel will do it in his address.

24. As stated above, being unwell due to severe headache, I did not even go to the prayer-ground. Apte returned to the Marina Hotel at about 6-00 p.m. and informed me that he had a view of the prayer meeting and would be in a position to stage the demonstration in a day or two. After about an hour, we heard some commotion at Gandhiji's prayer meeting due to an explosion and we further heard of an arrest, of a refugee. Apte thought it advisable to leave Delhi immediately and we left accordingly. It is not true that I met Badge at Hindu Sabha Bhavan on 20th January 1948. Several witnesses have deposed about my being at the Birla House on the 20th January, 1948; but I emphatically say that they are grossly mistaken in saying so. I submit that they are confusing my presence with somebody else's. The identification by some of these witnesses is utterly unreliable in view of the fact that I had not been to the Birla House on that day. These witnesses have identified me as I was shown to many of them by the Police while I was kept at Tughlak Road Police Station.

Further it was easy to identify me on account of the bandage over my head which remained up to the 12th of February 1948. The Police witnesses who have deposed to the contrary have perjured themselves and I have made a complaint at the very first identification parade in respect of the Delhi witnesses held in Bombay about this.

25. After a deliberate consideration of our future plan of staging the demonstration at Delhi in the prayer- meeting of Gandhiji; I very reluctantly consented to join Mr. Apte. It was not possible to get willing and able volunteers from Bombay and Poona under the new situation. Besides all our funds were exhausted and we were not in a position to spend for the batch of volunteers from Bombay to Delhi and back. We, therefore, decided to proceed to Gwalior and see Dr. Parchure who had under him to volunteers of Hindu Rashtra Sena. It was also a more or less economical plan to take volunteers from Gwalior to Delhi. We therefore started for Gwalior, after reaching Delhi by plane on the 27th of January 1948, by the night train reaching Gwalior very early morning. As it was dark at the time, we halted in a Dharamshala near the Station and in the morning, we saw Dr. Parchure at his residence. He was in a hurry to go to his dispensary. He asked us to see him in the afternoon. We saw him at about 4 p.m. and we found that he did not wish to help us and that his Volunteers were busy in local affairs. Completely disappointed I asked Apte to go back to Bombay or Poona and try for volunteers there and I came back to Delhi telling Apte that I would myself try for volunteers from

amongst the refugees. I deny categorically and with all the emphasis at my command that Mr. Apte and myself had been to Gwalior to secure a revolver or a pistol, as a number of such revolvers were being offered for sale clandestinely. Having reached Delhi in great despair, I visited the refugee camps at Delhi. While moving in the camps, my thoughts took a definite and final turn.

Chancily I came across a refugee who was dealing in arms and he showed me the pistol. I was tempted to have it and I bought it from him. It is the pistol which I later used in the shots I fired. On coming to the Delhi Railway station, I spent the night of 29th thinking and re-thinking about my resolve to end the present chaos and further destruction of the Hindus. I shall now deal about my relations with Veer Savarkar in political and other matters of which the prosecution has made so much.

26. Born in a devotional Brahmin family, I instinctively came to revere Hindu religion, Hindu history and Hindu culture. I had been intensely proud of Hindudom as a whole. Nevertheless as I grew up I developed a tendency to free thinking unfettered by any superstitious allegiance to any 'ism', political or religious. That is why I worked actively for the eradication of untouchability and the caste system based on birth alone. I publicly joined anti-caste movements and maintained that all Hindus should be treated with equal status as to rights social and religious, and should be high or low on their merit alone and not through the accident of birth in a particular caste or

profession. I used publicly to take part in organized anti-caste dinners in which thousands of Hindus, Brahmins, Kshatriyas, Vaishyas, Chamars and Bhangis broke the caste rules and dined in the company of each other.

27. I have read the works of Dadabhai Naoroji, Vivekanand, Gokhale, and Tilak along with the books of ancient and modern history of India and some prominent countries in the world like England, France, America and Russia. Not only that, I studied tolerably well the current tenets of Socialism and Communism too. But above all I studied very closely whatever Veer Savarkar and Gandhiji had written and spoken, as to my mind, these two ideologies had contributed more to mould the thought and action of modern India during the last fifty years or so, than any other single factor had done.

28. All this reading and thinking brought me to believe that above all it was my first duty to serve the Hindudom and the Hindu people, as a patriot and even as a humanitarian. For, is it not true that to secure the freedom and to safeguard the just interests of some thirty crores of Hindus constituted the freedom and the well-being of one fifth of human race? This conviction led me naturally to devote myself to the new Hindu Sangathanist ideology and program which alone I came to believe, could win and preserve the national independence of Hindustan, my Motherland and enable her to render true service to humanity as well.

29. I have worked for several years in R.S.S. and subsequently joined the Hindu Mahasabha and volunteered myself to

fight as a soldier under its pan Hindu flag. About this time Veer Savarkar was elected to the President ship of the Hindu Mahasabha. The Hindu Sangathan Movement got verify electrified and vivified as never before, under his magnetic lead and whirl-wind propaganda. Millions of Hindu Sangathanists looked up to him as the chosen hero, as the ablest and most faithful advocate of Hindu cause. I too was one of them. I worked devotedly to carry on the Mahasabha activities and hence came to be personally acquainted with Savarkarji.

30. Later on my friend and co-worker in the Hindu cause, Mr. Apte and myself decided to start a daily paper devoted to Hindu Sangathan Movement. We met a number of prominent Hindu Sangathanist leaders and after securing sympathy and financial help from them met Veer Savarkar as the President if the Mahasabha. He too sympathized with our project and advanced a sum of rupees fifteen thousand as his quota to the capital required, on condition that a limited company should be registered at our earliest convenience, and his advance should be transformed into so many shares.

31. Accordingly, we started the Daily Marathi paper 'Daily Agrani' and after some period a limited company was registered. The sums advanced by Veer Savarkar and others were converted into shares of Rs. 500 each. Amongst the directors and donors were such leading and respected gentlemen as Seth Gulab Chand (a brother of Shriman Seth Walchand Hirachandji), Mr. Shingre, an ex-

Minister of Bhor, Shreeman Bhalji Pendharkar, the film magnate of Kolhapur and others. Mr. Apte and I were the Managing Directors of the Company.

I was the editor solely responsible for the policy of the paper. We conducted the paper for years on strictly constitutional lines, and pleaded the policy of Hindu Sangathan in general.

32. As press representatives of this daily, Mr. Apte and me used to visit the Hindu Sangathan Office situated at Veer Savarkar's house in the middle hall on the ground floor of that house. This Hindu Sangathan Office was in the charge of Mr. G.V. Damle, the Secretary to Veer Savarkar and Mr. Appa Kasar, Veer Savarkar's body-guard. We used to visit this office to secure from Mr. Damle, the Secretary, public statements issued by Veer Savarkar for the Press in general to note down other important information about the President's tours, interviews etc. which his Secretary was authorized to publish. Mr. A. S. Bhide, who used to edit an English Weekly namely 'Free Hindustan' was also residing with his family as a tenant in a set of rooms on the same, ground-floor. The second reason why Mr. Apte and I used to visit Savarkar Sadan was to see Messers Bhide, Damle, Kasar and other Hindu Sabha workers who used to gather at the Hindu Sangathan Office and had been personal friends to each other.

To meet them all and have friendly chats, whenever we went to Bombay, we used to go to this office. Sometimes we used to discuss there the Hindu Sangathan work with them. Some of them used to help us in securing advertisements for our paper.

33. But it must be specially noted that these our casual visits to Savarkar Sadan were restricted generally to this Hindu Sangathan Office, situated on the ground floor, for the above-mentioned reasons. Veer Savarkar was residing on the first floor of the house. It was only very rarely that we could interview Veer Savarkar personally and that too by special appointment.

34. Some three years ago, Veer Savarkar's health got seriously impaired and since than he was generally confined to bed. He thereafter suspended all his public activities and more or less retired from public life. Thus deprived of his virile leadership and magnetic influence, the activities and influence of the Hindu Mahasabha too got crippled and when Dr. Mookerjee became its President the Mahasabha was actually reduced to the position of a hand-maid to the Congress. It became quite incapable of counteracting the dangerous anti-Hindu activities of Gandhite cabal on the one hand and the Muslim League on the other. Seeing this I lost all hope in the efficiency of the policy of running the Hindu Sangathan movement on the constitutional lines of the Mahasabha and began to shift myself. I determined to organise a youthful band of Hindu Sangathanists and adopt a fighting program both against the Congress and the League without consulting any of those prominent but old leaders of the Mahasabha.

35. I shall just mention here two striking instances only out of a number of them which painfully opened my eyes

about this time to the fact that Veer Savarkar and other old leaders of Mahasabha could no longer be relied upon by me and the Hindu youths of my persuasion to guide or even to appreciate the fighting program with which we aimed to counteract Gandhiji's activities inside and the Muslim League outside. In 1946 or thereabout the Muslim atrocities perpetrated on the Hindus under the Government patronage of Surhawardy in Noakhali, made our blood boil. Our shame and indignation knew no bounds, when we saw that Gandhiji had come forward to shield that very Surhawardy and began to style him as 'Shahid Saheb-a Martyr Soul (I) even in his prayer meetings. Not only that but after coming to Delhi, Gandhiji began to hold his prayer meetings in a Hindu temple in Bhangi Colony and persisted in reading passages from Quran as a part of the prayer in that Hindu temple in spite of the protest of the Hindu worshippers there. Of course he dared not read the Geeta in a mosque in the teeth of Muslim opposition. He knew what a terrible Muslim reaction would have been if he had done so. But he could safely trample over the feelings of the tolerant Hindu. To belie this belief, I determined to prove to Gandhiji that the Hindu too could be intolerant when his honor was insulted.

36. Mr. Apte and I decided to stage a series of demonstrations in Delhi at his meetings and make it impossible for him to hold such prayers. Mr. Apte with a large section of the refugees took out a procession in Delhi condemning Gandhiji and his Shahid Surhawardy and rushed into

his prayer-meeting in the Bhangi Colony. Seeing the tumultuous protest that followed, Gandhiji slyly took shelter behind barred and guarded doors although at that time we had not the slightest idea of using any force.

37. But when Veer Savarkar read the report of this demonstration, instead of appreciating our move, he called me and blamed me privately for such anarchical tactics, even though this demonstration was peaceful. He said just as I condemn the Congressites for breaking up your party meetings and election booths by disorderly conduct, I ought to condemn any such undemocratic conduct on the part of Hindu Sangathanist also. If Gandhiji preached anti-Hindu teachings in his prayer meetings you should hold your party meetings and condemn his teachings. Amongst ourselves all different parties should, conduct their propaganda on strictly constitutional lines."

38. The second leading incident took Place just after this, when the partition of India was actually decided on. A group of Hindu Mahasabhaites wanted to know what the Hindu Mahasabha's attitude should be with regard to the Congress Government which was certain to be the Government of the New State, ruling over the so-called India State in the remaining Part of India. Veer Savarkar and other top-ranking Hindu Mahasabha leaders quickly and emphatically said that any Indian Government formed to conduct such a freed Indian State should be no longer looked upon as a Government of a party – a Congress Government – but must be honored and obeyed

as a National Government of Hindustan and howsoever they deplored the creation of Pakistan their future motto should be a loyal and all-out support to the newly born Free Indian State. Thus, alone would it be possible to safeguard the newly won Freedom. Any attempt on their part to undermine the Indian State would bring in a Civil War and enable the Muslims to realize their sinful and secret mission to turn the whole of India into Pakistan.

39. My friends and I however returned unconvinced. We felt in our heart of hearts that time had come when we should bid good-bye to Veer Savarkar's lead and cease to consult him in our future policy and program, nor should we confide to him our future plans.

40. Just after that followed the terrible outburst of Muslim fanaticism in the Punjab and other parts of India. The Congress Government began to persecute, prosecute, and shoot the Hindus themselves who dared to resist the Muslim forces in Bihar, Calcutta, Punjab, and other places. Our worst fears seemed to be coming true; and yet how painful and disgraceful it was for us to find that the 15th of August 1947 was celebrated with illumination and festivities, while the whole of the Punjab was set by the Muslims in flames and Hindu blood ran rivers. The Hindu Mahasabhaites of my persuasion decided to boycott the festivities and the Congressite Government and to launch a fighting program to check Muslim onslaughts.

41. The meetings of the Working Committee of the Hindu Mahasabha and the All-India Hindu Convention were

held on or about 9th of August 1947, in Delhi, and Veer Savarkar presided. Mr. Apte and other friends and I wanted to make a last effort to bring the Mahasabha and its veteran leaders like Veer Savarkar, Dr. Mookerjee, Mr. L. B. Bhopatkar and others to our views and to adopt a fighting resolution. The Mahasabha Working Committee did not accept our suggestion to appoint a council of action against Hyderabad or boycott the Congress Government which was to run the newly created State of Divided India. To my mind to recognize a State of Divided India was tantamount to be a party to the cursed vivisection of India.

But instead, the Working Committee passed a frothy resolution and asked people to hoist the Bhagwa Flag on their houses on the day of August 15th, 1947. Veer Savarkar went further and actually insisted that the tricolor flag with the wheel should be recognized as a National Flag. We openly resented his attitude.

42. Not only that but on the 15th August, Veer Savarkar setting aside the will of the majority of Hindu Sangathanists hoisted this new flag with the wheel, as a National Flag, on his house along with the Bhagwa. In addition to that when Dr. Mookerji asked his permission through a trunk call to Veer Savarkar, as to whether Dr. Mookerji should accept a portfolio in the Indian Union Ministry, Veer Savarkar emphatically replied that the new Government must be recognized as a National Government whatever may be the elected party leading it, and must be supported by all

patriots and consequently Hindu Sangathanists ought to extend co-operation by accepting a portfolio if called upon to do so. He also congratulated the Congressite Ministers for the compromising attitude they were talking in calling on a Hindu Sabha leader like Dr. Mookerji to participate in the forming of the National Ministry, Mr. Bhopatkar too supported Dr. Mookerji.

43. By this time it came to light that some top leaders of the Congress and some of their Provincial Ministers too had contacted Veer Savarkar and there was a brisk correspondence between them for forming a united front to support the new State, which policy Veer Savarkar had already advocated. I myself could not be opposed to a common front of patriots, but while the Congress Government continued to be so sheepishly under the thumb of Gandhiji and while Gandhiji could thrust his anti-Hindu fads on that Congressite Government by resorting to such a simple trick as threatening a fast, it was clear to me that any common front under such circumstances was bound to be another form of setting up Gandhiji's Dictatorship and consequently a betrayal of Hindudom.

44. Every one of these steps taken by Veer Savarkar were so deeply resented by me that I myself along with Mr. Apte and some of the Young Hindu Sangathanist friends decided once for all to chalk and work out our active program quite independently of the Maha Sabha or its old veteran leaders. We resolved not to confide any of our new plans to any of them including Veer Savarkar.

45. I began to criticise the Hindu Maha Sabha and the policy of its old leaders in my daily paper 'Agrani' or 'Hindu Rashtra' and to openly call upon the young generation of Hindu Sangathanists to accept our own active program.

46. In order to work out my new independent program I decided to undertake two definite items, in hand to begin with. The first item was to organise a series of powerful though peaceful demonstrations against Gandhiji so as to make him feel the impact of organised Hindu discontent, and to create confusion and disorder by demonstrative protests, etc. in his obnoxious prayer-meetings through which he then carried out his anti-Hindu propaganda; and secondly to carry on an agitation against the Hyderabad State to defend our Hindu brothers and sisters near about the frontier line from the fanatic atrocities committed, on them by the Muslims. As such a program could only be carried out on secret and dictatorial lines we resolved to divulge it only to those who believed in it and would obey our orders without questioning.

47. I would not have referred to the above details in this statement but for the learned prosecutor's opening speech in which be painted me as a mere tool in the hands of Veer Savarkar. This statement I felt to be a deliberate insult to my independence of judgment and action.

The above facts had to be mentioned to dispel the incorrect impression about me, if any. Consequently, before I begin to narrate the rest of my statement, I re-assert that it is not true that Veer Savarkar had any knowledge of my activities which ultimately led me to fire shots at Gandhiji; I repeat that it is not true and it is totally false that either Mr. Apte in my presence or I myself told Badge that Veer Savarkar had given us an order to finish Gandhiji, Nehru and Suhrawardy as the approver is made to state falsely. It is not true that, we ever took Badge to Veer Savarkar's house to take the last Darshan of Veer Savarkar in connection with any such plot or that Veer Savarkar ever said to us, "Be successful and come back. *Yashasvi houn ya.*" Neither Mr. Apte in my presence nor I myself ever told Badge that Veer Savarkar told us that Gandhiji's hundred years were over and therefore we were bound to be successful. I was neither so superstitious as to crave such blessings, nor so childish as to believe in such fortune-telling.

48. The back-ground to the event of the 30th January, 1948 was wholly and exclusively political and I would like to explain it at some length. The fact that Gandhiji honored the religious books of Hindus. Muslims and others or that he used to recite during his prayers verses from the Geeta, the Quran and Bible never provoked any ill will in me towards him. To my mind it is not at all objectionable to study comparative religion. Indeed, it is a merit.

49. The territory bounded by the North Western Frontier in North and Cape Comorin in the South and the areas between Karachi and Assam that is the whole of pre-partition India has always been to me my mother-land. In this vast area live people of various faiths and I hold

that these creeds should have full and equal freedom for following their ideals and beliefs. In this area the Hindus are the most numerous. They have no place which they can call their own beyond or outside this, country. Hindustan is thus both motherland and the holy land for the Hindus from times immemorial. To the Hindus largely this country owes its fame and glory, its culture and art, knowledge, science and philosophy. Next to the Hindus the Muslims are numerically predominant. They made systematic inroads into this country since the 10th century and gradually succeeded in establishing Muslim rule over the greater part of India.

50. Before the advent of the British both Hindus and Muslims as a result of centuries of experience had come to realize that the Muslims could not remain as masters in India; nor could they be driven away. Both had clearly understood that both had come to stay. Owing to the rise of the Maharattas, the revolt of the Rajputs and the uprising of the Sikhs, the Muslim hold on the country had become very feeble and although some of them continued to aspire for supremacy in India, practical people could see clearly that such hopes were futile. On the other hand the British had proved more powerful in battle and in intrigue than either the Hindus or Musalmans, and by their adoption of improved methods of administration and the assurance of the security of the life and property without any discrimination both the Hindus and the Muslims accepted them as inevitable.

Differences between the Hindus and the Muslims did exist even before the British came. Nevertheless, it is a fact that the British made the most unscrupulous use of these differences and created more differences in order to maintain their power and authority. The Indian National Congress which was started with the object of winning power for the people in the governance of the country had from the beginning kept before it the ideal of complete nationalism which implies that all Indians should enjoy equal rights and complete equality on the basis of democracy. This ideal of removing the foreign rule and replacing it by the democratic power and authority of the people appealed to me most from the very start of my public career.

51. In my writings and speeches I have always advocated that the religious and communal consideration should be entirely eschewed in the public affairs of the country, at elections, inside and, outside the legislatures and in the making and unmaking of Cabinets. I have throughout stood for a secular State with joint electorates and to my mind this is the only sensible thing to do. (Here I read parts of the resolutions passed at the Bilaspur Session of the Hindu Mahasabha held in December, 1944. Annexure Pages 12 and 13), Under the influence of the Congress this ideal was steadily making headway amongst the Hindus. But the Muslims as a community first stood aloof and later on under the corroding influence of the Divide and Rule Policy of the foreign masters were encouraged to cherish the ambition of dominating the Hindus. The first indication

of this outlook was the demand for separate electorates instigated by the then Viceroy Lord Minto in 1906. The British Government accepted this demand under the excuse of minority protection. While the Congress party offered a verbal opposition, it progressively supported separatism by ultimately adopting the notorious formula of neither accepting nor rejecting in 1934.

52. Thus had originated and intensified the demand for the disintegration of this country. What was the thin end of the wedge in the beginning became Pakistan in the end. The mistake however was begun with the laudable object of bringing out a united front amongst all classes in India in order to drive out the foreigner and it was hoped that separatism would eventually disappear.

53. In spite of my advocacy of joint electorates in principle I reconciled myself with the temporary introduction of separate electorates since the Muslims were keen on them. I however insisted that representation should be granted in strict proportion to the number of every community and no more. I have, uniformly maintained this stand.

54. Under the inspiration of our British masters on the one hand and the encouragement by the Congress under Gandhiji's leadership on the other, the Muslim League went on increasing its demands on Communal basis. The Muslim community continuously backed the Muslim League; each successive election proved that the Muslim League was able to bank on the fanaticism and ignorance of the Muslim masses and the League was thus encouraged,

in its policy of separatism on an over increasing scale year after year.

55. As I have shown before despite their objection to the principle of communal electorates the unreasonable demands of the Muslim League were, conceded by the Congress – firstly by the Lucknow Pact of 1916 and at each successive revision of the constitution thereafter.

This lapse from nationalism and democracy on the part of the Congress has proved an expensive calamity as the sequel has shown.

56. Since the year 1920, that is to say after the dismissal of Lokamanya Tilak, Gandhiji's influence in the Congress first increased and then became supreme. His activities for public awakening were phenomenal in their intensity and were reinforced by the slogan of truth and non-violence which he ostentatiously paraded before the country. No sensible or enlightened person could object to these, slogans; in fact, there is nothing new or original in them. They are implicit in every constitutional public movement. To imagine that the bulk of mankind can ever become capable of scrupulous adherence to these lofty principles in its normal life from day to day is a mere dream. In fact, honor, duty and love of one's own kith and kin and country might often compel us to disregard non-violence. I could never conceive that an armed resistance to the aggressor is unjust. I will consider it a religious and moral duty to resist and if possible, to overpower such an enemy by the use of force. Shree Ramchandra

killed Ravan in a tumultuous fight and relieved Sita. Shree Krishna killed Kansa to end his wickedness. In the Mahabharat Arjun had to fight and slay, quite a number of his friends and relations including the revered Bhishma, because the latter was on the side of the aggressor. It is my firm belief that in dubbing Rama, Krishna and Arjuna as guilty of violence is to betray a total ignorance of the springs of human action. It was the heroic fight put up by the Chhatrapati Shivaji Maharaj that first checked and eventually destroyed Muslim tyranny in India. It was absolutely correct tactics for Shivaji to kill Afzal Khan as the latter would otherwise have surely killed him. In condemning Shivaji, Rana Pratap and Guru Govind as misguided patriots, Gandhiji has merely exposed his self-conceit.

57. Each of the heroes in his time resisted aggression on our country, protected the people against the atrocities and outrages by alien fanatic and won back the motherland from the invader. On the other hand, during more than thirty years of the undisputed leadership of the Mahatma there were more desecration of temples, more forcible and fraudulent conversions, more outrages on women and finally the loss of one third of the country. It is therefore astounding that his followers cannot see what is clear even to the blind, viz. that the Mahatma was a mere pigmy before Shivaji, Rana Pratap and Guru Govind. His condemnation of these illustrious heroes was to say the least, most presumptuous.

58. The clique which has got into power with the patronage of British imperialism by a cowardly surrender to the Partition of India at the point of Muslim violence is now trying to exploit Gandhiji's death in hundred hectic ways for its own selfish aims. But history will give to them their proper place in the niche of fame. Gandhiji was, paradoxical as it may appear, a violent pacifist who brought untold calamities on the country in the name of truth and nonviolence, while Rana Pratap, Shivaji and the Guru will remain enshrined in the hearts of their countrymen forever and for the freedom they brought to them.

59. As pointed out herein below Gandhiji's political activities can be conveniently divided under three heads. He returned to India from England some time about the end of 1914 and plunged into the public life of the country almost immediately. Unfortunately, soon after his arrival Sir Pherozeshah Mehta and Mr. G. K. Gokhale, the latter whom Gandhiji called his Guru, died within a short span of time. Gandhiji began his work by starting an Ashram in Ahmedabad on the banks of the Sabarmati river, and made Truth and Nonviolence his slogans. He had often acted contrary to his professed principles and if it was for appeasing the Muslim he hardly had any scruple in doing so. Truth and Non-violence are excellent as an ideal and admirable as guides in action. They are, however, to be practiced in actual day-to-day life and not in the air. I am showing later on that Gandhiji himself was guilty of glaring breaches of his much-vaunted ideals.

Gandhiji's political career will be divided as already stated under three heads

(I) The period between 1915 to 1939-40.

(II) The period between 1939-40 to 3rd June, 1947, when the Indian National Congress, surrendered to Mr. Jinnah and accepted, Pakistan under the leadership of the Mahatma.

(Ill) The period between the date of partition to the day of his last fast unto death resulting in the payment of Rs. 55 crores to Pakistan and the Mahatma's death within a short period.

61. When Gandhiji finally returned to India at the end of 1914, he brought with him a very high reputation for courageous leadership of Indians in South Africa. He had placed himself at the head of the struggle for the assertion and vindication of the national self-respect of India and for our rights of citizenship against white tyranny in that country. He was honored and obeyed by Hindus, Muslims and Parsis alike and was universally acclaimed as the leader of all Indians in South Africa. His simplicity of life, his unselfish devotion to the cause which, he had made his own, his self-sacrifice and earnestness in fighting against the racial arrogance of the Afrikaners had raised the prestige of Indians. In India he had endeared himself to all.

62. When he returned here to serve his countrymen in their struggle for freedom, he had legitimately hoped that as in Africa he would command the unchallenged confidence

and respect of all communities. But in this hope he soon found himself disappointed.

India was not South Africa. In South Africa, Indians had claimed nothing but elementary rights of citizenship which were denied to them. They had all, a common and acute grievance. The Boer and the British both had treated them like door mats. Hindus, Muslims and Parsis therefore stood united like one man against the common enemy. They had no other quarrel with the South African Government. The Indian problem at home was quite different. We were fighting for home rule, self-Government and even for Independence. We were intent on overthrowing an Imperial Power, which was determined to continue its sway over us by all possible means including the policy of 'Divide and Rule' which had intensified the cleavage between the Hindus and Muslims. Gandhiji was thus confronted at the very outset with a problem the like of which he had never experienced in South Africa. Indeed, in South Africa he had smooth sailing throughout. The identity of interest between the various communities there was complete and every Indian had ranged himself behind him. But in India communal franchise, separate electorates and the like had already undermined the solidarity of the nation, more of such were in the offing and the sinister policy of communal favoritism was being pursued by the British with the utmost tenacity without any scruple. Gandhiji therefore, found it most difficult to obtain the unquestioned leadership of the Hindus and the Muslims in India as in South Africa.

But he had been accustomed to be the leader of all Indians and quite frankly he could not understand the leadership of a divided country.

It was absurd for his honest mind to think of accepting the generalship of an army divided against itself.

63. For the first five years after his return to India there was not much scope for the attainment by him of supreme leadership in Indian politics. Dadabhai Naoroji, Sir Pherozeshah Mehta, Lokmanya Tilak and Mr. G. K. Gokhale and others were still alive and Gandhiji honored as he was popular as he was, was still a junior compared to those veterans both in age and experience. But an inexorable fate removed all of them in five years and with the death of Lokmanya Tilak in August 1920, Gandhiji was at once thrown into the front fine.

64. He saw that the foreign rulers by the policy of 'Divide and Rule' wore corrupting the patriotism of the Muslims and that there was little chance of his leading a united host to the battle for Freedom unless he was able to cement fellow feeling and common devotion to the Motherland. He, therefore, made Hindu-Muslim Unity the foundation of his politics. As a counterblast to the British tactics he started making the most friendly approaches to the Muslim community and reinforced them by making generous and extravagant promises to the Muslims. This, of course, was not wrong in itself so long as it was done consistently with India's struggle for democratic national freedom; but Gandhiji completely forgot this, the most essential aspect

of his campaign for unity, with what results we all know by now.

65. Our British rulers were able, out of Indian resource continuously, to make concessions to Muslims and to keep the various communities divided. By 1919 Gandhiji had become desperate in his endeavors to get the Muslims to trust him and went from one absurd promise to another. He promised ‘a blank cheque’ to the Muslims. He backed the Khilafat movement in this country and was able to enlist the full support of the National Congress in that policy.

For a time, Gandhiji appeared to succeed and prominent Muslim leaders in India became his followers; Mr. Jinnah was nowhere in 1920-21, and the Ali Brothers became de facto Muslim leaders.

Gandhiji welcomed this as the coming promise of leadership, of the Muslims. He made most of the Ali Brothers, raised them to the skies by flattery and unending concessions; but what he wanted never happened. The Muslims and the Khilafat Committee as a distinct political religious organization and throughout maintained it as a separate entity from the Congress; and very soon the Moplah Rebellion showed that the Muslims had not the slightest idea of national unity on which Gandhiji had set his heart and had stakes so much. There followed as usual in such cases, a huge slaughter of the Hindus, numerous forcible conversions, rape and arson. The British Government entirely unmoved by the rebellion suppressed it in a few months and left to Gandhiji the joy of his Hindu-Muslim Unity. The Khilafat agitation had failed and let down Gandhiji. British Imperialism emerged stronger, the Muslims became more fanatical and the consequences were visited on the Hindus. But undaunted by the tactics of the British Rulers, Gandhiji became more stubborn in the pursuit of his phantom of Hindu-Muslim Unity. By the Act of 1919 separate electorates were enlarged and communal representation was continued not merely in the legislature and the local bodies but even extended within the Cabinet. The services began to be distributed on the communal basis and the Muslims obtained high jobs from our British Masters not on merit but by remaining aloof from the struggle for freedom and because of their being the followers of Islam. Government patronage to Muslims in the name of Minority protection penetrated throughout the body-politic of the Indian State and the Mahatma's meaningless slogans were no match against this wholesale corruption of the Muslim mind. But Gandhiji did not relent. He still lived in the hope of being the common leader both of the Hindus and Muslims and the more he was defeated, the more he indulged in encouraging the Muslims by extravagant methods. The position continued to deteriorate and by 1925 it became patent to all that the Government had won all along the line; but like the proverbial gambler Gandhiji increased his stake. He agreed to the separation of Sind and to the creation of a separate province in the N. W. Frontier. He also went on conceding one undemocratic demand after another to the Muslim League in the vain hope of enlisting its support in the national struggle. By this time the stock of the Ali Brothers had gone down and Mr. Jinnah who had staged a come-back was having the best of both the worlds. Whatever concessions the Government and the Congress made, Mr. Jinnah accepted and asked for more. Separation of Sind from Bombay and the creation of the N. W. Frontier were followed by the Round Table Conference in which the minority question loomed large. Mr. Jinnah stood out against the federation until Gandhiji himself requested Mr. McDonald, the Labor Premier, to give the Communal Award. Further seeds were thereby sown for the disintegration of this country. The communal principle became deeply impeded in the Reforms of 1935. Mr. Jinnah took the fullest advantage of every situation.

The Federation of India which was to consolidate Indian Nationhood was in fact, defeated; Mr. Jinnah had never taken kindly to it. The Congress continued to support the Communal Award under the very hypocritical words of neither supporting nor opposing, which really meant its tacit acceptance. During the War 1939-44, Mr. Jinnah took up openly one attitude – a sort of benevolent neutrality – and promised to support the war as soon as the Muslims rights were conceded; in April 1940, within six months of the War, Mr. Jinnah came out with the demand for Pakistan on the basis of his two-nation theory. Mr. Jinnah totally ignored the fact that there were Hindus and Muslims in large numbers in every part of India. There may be a majority of Hindus in some case and a minority of Muslims in other Provinces and vice versa, but there was no Province in India where either the Hindus or the Muslims were negligible in numbers and that any division of India would leave the minority question wholly unsolved.

66. The British Government liked the Pakistan idea as it kept the Hindus and Muslims estranged during the war and thereby avoided embarrassing the Government. The Muslims did not obstruct the war efforts and the Congress sometimes remained neutral and sometimes opposed. On the other hand, the Hindu Sabha realized that this was an opportunity for our young men to have a military training, which is absolutely essential for our nation, and from which we were rather kept far away intentionally by the British. But due to this war the doors of Army, Navy and Air-force were opened to us, and Mahasabha urged our countrymen to militarize Hindus. The result was that nearly 1/2 millions of Hindus learnt the art of war and mastered the mechanized aspect of modern warfare. The Congress Governments are enjoying the fruits of the Mahasabha's foresight because the troops they are using in Kashmir and had employed in Hyderabad would not have been there readymade but for the effort of men with such outlook. The Congress in 1942, started the Quit India' movement in the name of Freedom; violent outrages ware perpetrated by Congress men in every Province. In the Province of North Bihar there was hardly a railway station which was not burnt or destroyed by the Congress non-co-operators; but in spite of all the opposition of the

Congress the Germans were beaten in April, 1945 and the Japanese in August, 1945. The atomic bomb brought the collapse of the Japanese resistance and the British won against Japanese and Germans in spite of the opposition of the Congress party. The 'Quit India' campaign of 1942 had completely failed.

Britishers had triumphed and the Congress leaders decided to come to terms with them. Indeed in the subsequent years the Congress policy can be quite correctly described as 'Peace at any Price' and 'Congress in Office at all costs.' The Congress compromised with the British who placed it in office and in return the Congress surrendered to the violence of Mr. Jinnah, carved out one-third of India to him an explicitly racial and theological State and destroyed two million human beings in the process. Pandit Nehru now professes again and again that the Congress stands for a secular State and violently denounces those who reminded him that only last year he agreed to a communal and theological State; his vociferous adherence to a Secular State is nothing but a case of 'my lady protests too much.'

67. The 'Quit India' movement had to be abandoned, the Congress support to the war against Japan had to be assured and the Viceroy Lord Wavell had to be accepted as the head of the Government of India before the Congress was to be called into the Conference Chamber.

68. This section summarizes the back-ground of the agony of India's partition and the tragedy of Gandhiji's

assassination. Neither the one nor the other gives me any pleasure to record or to remember, but the Indian people and the world at large ought to know the history of the last thirty years during which India has been torn into pieces by the Imperialist policy of the British and under a mistaken policy of communal unity. The Mahatma was betrayed into action which has ultimately led not to the Hindu-Muslim Unity but to the shattering of the whole basis of that Five crores of Indian Muslims have ceased to be our countrymen; virtually the non-Muslim minority in Western Pakistan have been liquidated either by the most brutal murders or by a forced tragic removal from their moorings of centuries; the same process is furiously at work in Eastern Pakistan.

One hundred and ten millions of people have become torn from their homes of which not less than four millions are Muslims and when I found that even after such terrible results Gandhiji continued to pursue the same policy of appeasement, my blood boiled, and I could not tolerate him any longer. I do not mean to use hard words against Gandhiji personally nor do I wish to conceal my utter dissent from and disapproval of the very foundation of his policy and methods.

Gandhiji in fact succeeded in doing what the British always wanted to do in pursuance of their policy of Divide and Rule'. He helped them in dividing India and it is not yet certain whether their rule has ceased.

69. The accumulating provocation of 32 years culminating in his last pro-Muslim fast at last goaded me to the conclusion

that the existence of Gandhiji should be brought to an end immediately. On coming back to India he developed a subjective mentality under which he alone was to be the final judge of what was right or wrong. If the country wanted his leadership it had to accept his infallibility, if it did not, he would stand aloof from the Congress and carry on in his own way. Against such an attitude there can be no half way house; either the Congress had to surrender its will to his and had to be content with playing the second fiddle to all his eccentricity, whimsicality, metaphysics and primitive vision, or it had to carry on without him. He alone was the judge of every one and everything; he was the master brain guiding the civil disobedience movement; nobody else knew the technique of that movement; he alone knew when to begin it and when to withdraw it.

The movement may succeed or fail; it may bring untold disasters and political reverses but that could make no difference to the Mahatma's infallibility. 'A Satyagrahi can never fail' was his formula for declaring - his own infallibility and nobody except himself knew who a Satyagrahi was. Thus Gandhiji became the judge and the counsel in his own case. These childish inanities and obstinacies coupled with a most severe austerity of life, ceaseless work and lofty character made Gandhiji formidable and irresistible. Many people thought his politics were irrational but they had either to withdraw from the Congress or to place their intelligence at his feet to do what he liked with it. In a position of such absolute irresponsibility Gandhiji was guilty of blunder after blunder, failure after failure and disaster after disaster.

No one single political victory can be claimed to his credit during 33 years of his political predominance. Herein below I mention in some detail the series of blunders which he committed during 32 years of his undisputed leadership.

70. I shall now describe briefly the enormous mischief done by the slogans and the nostrums which Gandhiji prescribed and followed, in pursuance of his policy, the fatal results that we now know. Here are some of them:

(a) Khilafat – As a result of the First World War, Turkey had lost most of its Empire in Africa and the Middle East. It had lost all its European Imperial possessions also and by 1914 only a strip of land was all that was left to her on the continent of Europe. The young Turks had forced the Sultan of Turkey to abdicate and with the disappearance of the Sultan the Khilafat was also abolished. The Indian Muslims' devotion to the Khilafat was strong and earnest and they believed that is was Britain that had brought about the downfall of the Sultan and the Khilafat. They therefore started a campaign for the revival of the Khilafat. In the moment of opportunism the Mahatma misconceived the idea that by helping the Khilafat Movement he would become the leader of the Muslims in India as he already was of the Hindus and that with the Hindu-Muslim Unity thus achieved the British would soon have to concede Swaraj. But again, Gandhiji miscalculated and by leading the Indian National Congress to identify itself with the Khilafat Movement, he quite gratuitously introduced theological element which has proved a tragic and expensive calamity. For the moment the movement for the revival of the Khilafat appeared to be succeeding. The Muslims who were not with the Khilafat Movement soon became out of date and the Ali Brothers who were its foremen leaders swam on the crest of a wave of popularity and carried everything before them. Mr. Jinnah found himself a lonely figure and was of no consideration for a few years. The movement however failed. Our British Masters were not unduly shaken and as a combined result of repression and the Montague Chelmsford Reforms they were able to tide over the Khilafat Movement in a few years' time. The Muslims had kept the Khilafat Movement distinct from the Congress all along; they welcomed the Congress support but they did not merge with it. When failure came the Muslims became desperate with disappointment and their anger was sited on the Hindus. Innumerable riots in the various parts of India followed the chief victims being the Hindus everywhere. The Hindu-Muslim Unity of the Mahatma became a mirage.

(b) Moplah Rebellion – Malabar, Punjab, Bengal and N. W. F. Province were the scene of repeated outrages on the Hindus. The Moplah rebellion as it was called was the most prolonged and concentrated attack on the Hindu religion, Hindu honor, Hindu life and Hindu property; hundreds of Hindus were forcibly converted to Islam, women were outraged. The Mahatma who had brought about this entire calamity on India by his communal policy kept mum. He never uttered a single word of reproach against the aggressors nor did he allow the Congress to take any active steps whereby repetition of such outrages could be prevented. On the other hand he went to the length of denying the numerous cases of forcible conversions in Malabar and actually published in his paper 'Young India' that there was only one case of forcible conversion. His own Muslim friends informed him that he was wrong and that the forcible conversions were numerous in Malabar. He never corrected his misstatements but went to the absurd length of starting a relief fund for the Moplahs instead of for their victims; but the Promised land of Hindu-Muslim Unity was not yet in sight.

(c) Afghan Amir Intrigue – When the Khilafat movement failed Ali Brothers decided to do something which might keep alive the Khilafat sentiments. Their slogan was that whoever was the enemy of the Khilafat was also the enemy of Islam and as the British were chiefly responsible for the defeat and the dethronement of the Sultan of Turkey, every faithful Muslim was in solemn duty bound to be a bitter enemy of Britain. With that object they secretly intrigued to invite the Amir or Afghanistan to invade India and promised him every support. There is a long history behind this intrigue; Ali brothers never denied their share in the conspiracy. The Mahatma pursued his tactics of getting Hindu-Muslim Unity by supporting the Ali brothers through thick and through thin. He publicly poured his affection on them and promised them unstinted support in the restoration of the Khilafat. Even with regard to the invasion of India by the Amir the Mahatma directly and indirectly supported the Ali Brothers. This is proved beyond the. shadow of a doubt. The late Mr. Shastri, Mr. C.Y. Chintamani the Editor or the 'Leader' of Allahabad and even the Mahatma's life-long friend, the late Rev. C. F. Andrews told him quite clearly that his speeches and writings amounted to a definite support to the Ali Brothers in their invitation to the Amir of Afghanistan to invade India. The following quotations from the Mahatma's Writing in those days should make it clear, that he had forgotten his own country in his one consuming desire to please the Muslims and had become a party to the invasion of his motherland by a foreign Ruler.

The Mahatma supported the invasion in the following words:

"I cannot understand why the Ali Brothers are going to be arrested as the rumors go, and why I am to remain free. They have done nothing which I would not do. If they had sent a message, to Amir, I also would send one to inform the Amir that if he came, no Indian so long as I can help it, would help the Government to drive him back."

The vigilance of the British broke the conspiracy nothing came out of the Ali Brothers' grotesque scheme of the invasion of India and Hindu-Muslim Unity remained as far away as before.

(d) (i) Attack on Arya Samaj – Gandhiji ostentatiously displayed his love for Muslims by a most unworthy and unprovoked attack on the Arya Samaj in 1924. He publicly denounced the Samaj for its supposed sins of omission and commission; it was an utterly unwarranted reckless and discreditable attack, but whatever would please the Mohammedans was the heart's desire of Gandhiji. The Arya Samaj made a powerful but polite retort and for some time Gandhiji was silenced, but the growing political influence of Gandhiji weakened the Arya Samaj. No follower of Swami Dayanand could Possibly be a Gandhian Congressman in politics. The two things are entirely incompatible; but the lure of office and Leadership has induced numerous Arya Samajists to play the double game of claiming to be Gandhi to Congressmen and Arya Samajists at the same time. The result was that a ban on Satyartha Prakash was imposed by the Government of Sind four years ago and the Arya Samaj on the whole took it lying down. As a result its hold on Hindu social and religious life has been further considerably crippled.

Individual members of the Samaj are and were strong nationalists. The late Lala Lajpat Rai, and

Swami Shradhanand to mention only two names ware staunch Arya Samajists but they were foremost amongst the leaders of the Congress till the end of their life. They did not stand for blind support to Gandhi, but were definitely opposed to his pro-Muslim Policy, and openly fought him on that issue. But these great men are gone now. We know that the bulk of the Arya Samaj continues to be what they always were, but they are ill-informed and badly led by the self-seeking section of the Samaj. The Samaj has ceased to be the force and the power that it was at one time.

(d) (ii) Gandhiji's attack did not improve his popularity with the Muslims but it provoked a Muslim youth to murder Swami Shraddhanandji within a few months. The charge against the Samaj that it was a reactionary body was manifestly false. Everybody knew that far from being reactionary body the Samaj had been vanguard of social reforms among the Hindus. The Samaj had for a hundred years stood for the abolition of untouchability long before the birth of Gandhiji. The Samaj had popularized widow remarriage. The Samaj had denounced the caste system, and preached the oneness of not merely the Hindus, but of all those who were prepared to follow its tenets. Gandhiji was completely silenced for some time but his leadership made people forget his baseless attack on the Arya Samaj and even weakened the Samaj to a large extent.

Swami Dayanand Saraswati who was the founder of the Arya Samaj; had no fad about violence or non-violence. In his teaching the use of force was not ruled out but was. permissible if morally desirable. It must have been a struggle for the leaders of the Arya Samaj whether to remain within the Congress or not. because Gandhiji insisted on non-violence in all cases and Swami Dayanand made no bones about it. But Swamiji was dead and Gandhiji's star was ascendant in the political firmament.

(e) Separation of Sind – By 1928 Mr. Jinnah's stock had risen very high and the Mahatma had already conceded many unfair and improper demands of Mr. Jinnah at the expense of Indian democracy and the Indian nation and the Hindus. The Mahatma even supported the separation of Sind from the Bombay Presidency and threw the Hindus of Sind to the communal wolves. Numerous riots took place in Sind-Karachi, Sukkur, Shikarpur and other places in which the Hindus were the only sufferers and the Hindu-Muslim Unity receded further from the horizon.

(f) League's Good Bye to Congress – With each defeat Gandhiji became even keener on his method of achieving Hindu-Muslim Unity. Like the gambler who had lost heavily he became more desperate increasing his stakes each time and indulged in the most irrational concessions, if only they could placate Mr. Jinnah and enlist his support under the Mahatma's leadership in the fight for freedom. But the aloofness of the Muslims from the Congress increased with the advance of years and the Muslim League refused to have anything to do with the Congress after 1928. The resolution of Independence passed by the Congress at its Lahore Session in 1929 found the Muslims conspicuous by their absence and strongly aloof from the Congress organization. The hope of Hindu Muslim Unity was hardly entertained by anybody thereafter; but Gandhiji continued to be resolutely optimistic and surrendered more and more to Muslim communalism.

(g) Round Table Conference and Communal Award – The British authorities both in India and in England, had realized that the demand for a bigger and truer installment of constitutional reforms was most insistent and claimant in India and that in spite of their unscrupulous policy of 'Divide and Rule' and the communal discord which it had generated, the resulting situation had brought them no permanence and security so far as British Rule in India was concerned. They therefore decided by the end of 1929 to convene a Round Table Conference in England early in the next year and made a declaration to that effect. Mr. Ramsay McDonald was the Prime Minister and a Labor Government was in power; but the action was too late. The resolution of Independence was passed a month later at the Lahore Session of the Congress in spite of the aforesaid declaration and the Congress Party decided to boycott this Round Table Conference. Instead, a Salt Campaign was started after a few months which created tremendous enthusiasm and nearly 70,000 people, went to jails in breaking the provisions of the Salt Act. The Congress however soon regretted its boycott of the First Round Table Conference and at the Karachi Congress of 1931 it was decided to send Gandhiji alone as the Congress Representative to Second Session of Round Table Conference. Anybody who reads the proceedings of that Session will realize that Gandhiji was the biggest factor in bringing about the total failure of the Conference. Not one of the decisions of the Round Table Conference was in support of democracy or nationalism and the Mahatma went to the length of inviting Mr. Ramsay McDonald to give what was called the Communal Award, thereby strengthening the disintegrating forces of communalism which had already corroded the body politic for 24 years past. The Mahatma was thus responsible for a direct and substantial intrusion of communal electorate and communal franchise in the future Parliament of India. There is no wonder that when the communal award was given by Mr. Ramsay MacDonald, the Mahatma refused to oppose it and the members of the Assembly were asked 'Neither to support nor to reject it.' Gandhiji himself put an axe on the communal unity on which he had staked so much for the previous, fifteen years. No wonder under the garb of minority protection we got in the Government of India Act of 1935 a permanent statutory recognition of communal franchise, communal electorate and even weightage for the minorities especially the Muslims, both in the, Provinces and in the Centre. Those elected on the communal franchise would be naturally communal minded and would have no interest in bridging the gulf between communalism and nationalism. The formation of a parliamentary party on political and, economic grounds thus became impossible. Hindus and Muslims became divided in opposite camps and worked as rival parties, placing increased momentum to separatism. Almost everywhere Hindus became victims of communal orgies at the hands of the Muslims. People became perfectly cynical about any possibility of unity between Hindus and Muslims but the Mahatma kept on repeating his barren formula all the time. (Here refer to Pandit Madan Mohan Malaviya's speech against the acceptance of Communal Award.)

(h) Acceptance of office and Resigning in Huff – Provincial Autonomy was introduced from the 1st of April, 1937 under the Government of India Act 1935. The act was bristling with safeguards, special Powers, protection to British personnel in the various services intact. The Congress therefore would not accept office at first but soon found out that in every Province a Ministry was constituted and that at least in five Provinces they were functioning in the normal manner. In the other six Provinces the Ministers were in a minority but they ware forging ahead with their nation building program and the Congress felt that it would be left out in the cold if it persisted in its policy of barren negation. It therefore decided to accept office in July, 1937; in doing so it committed a serious blunder in excluding the members of the Muslim League from effective participation in the Cabinet.

They only admitted into the Cabinet such Muslims as were congress-men. This was the right policy for a country with citizen franchise and without communal representation but having accepted communal electorate and communal franchise and other paraphernalia of separatism, it became untenable to keep out the members of Muslim League who represented the bulk of the Muslims in every province, where they were in a minority. The Nationalist Muslims who became Ministers were not representatives of the Muslims in the sense in which the Muslim League Members were and in not taking the League Members in the Cabinet the Congress openly repudiated its own action in statutorily having recognized itself communal by statute. On the other hand the Muslims were quite unwilling to come under the Congress control; their interest never needed protection. The Governors were there always ready and willing to offer the most sympathetic support, but the rejection of Muslim League Members as Ministers gave Mr. Jinnah a tactical advantage which he utilized to the full and in 1939 when the Congress resigned Office in a huff, it completely played in the hand of the Muslim League and British Imperialism. Under Section 93 of the Government of India Act 1935 the Governments of the Congress Provinces were taken over by the Governors and the Muslim League Ministries remained in power and authority in the remaining Provinces. The Governors carried on the administration with a definite leaning towards the Muslims as an Imperial Policy of Britain and communalism reigned right throughout the country through the Muslim Ministries on the one hand and the pro-Muslim Governors on the other. The Hindu-Muslim Unity of Gandhiji became a dream, if it were ever anything else; but Gandhiji never cared. His ambition was to become the leader of Hindu and Muslims alike and in resigning the Ministries the Congress again sacrificed democracy and nationalism. The fundamental rights of the Hindus, religious, political, economic and social, all were sacrificed at the altar of the Mahatmic obstinacy.

(i) League Taking Advantage of War – Encouraged by the situation thus created the Muslim Government in five Provinces and the pro-Muslim Governors in the other six, Mr. Jinnah went ahead in full speed. The congress opposed the war in one way or another. Mr. Jinnah and the League had a very clear policy. They remained neutral and created no trouble for the Government; but in the year following the Lahore Session of the Muslim League passed a resolution for the partition of India as a condition for their co-operation in the war. Lord Linlithgow within a few months of the Lahore Resolution gave full support to the Muslims in their policy of separation by a declaration of Government Policy which assured the Muslims that no change in the political constitution of India will be made without the consent of all the elements in India's national life. The Muslim League and Mr. Jinnah were thus vested with a veto over the political progress of this country by the pledge given by the Viceroy of India. From that day the progress of disintegration advanced with accumulated force. Muslims were not prohibited by the League from getting recruited to the Army, Navy and Air Force and they did so in large numbers. In fact the Punjab Muslims resented their percentage in the Indian Army at all reduced thus, with a view to preparing for eventualities in future Muslim State as is being done in Kashmir today, and of course the Muslim League never created any difficulty for the Government throughout the six years of the global war. (Here refer to the speech of the late Sir Sikandar Hyat Khan delivered at Cairo to the armed forces during the last World War) All that they wanted was that no changes should be made in the constitution of India without their full consent and that full consent could be obtained if only Pakistan was conceded. This assurance was virtually given by Lord Linlithgow in August, 1940.

(j) Cripp's Partition Proposal Accepted – The Congress did not know its own mind as to whether it should support the war, oppose or remain neutral. All these attitudes were expressed in turn one after the other; sometimes by way of speeches, sometimes by way of resolutions, sometimes through Press campaigns and sometimes in other ways. Government naturally felt that the Congress has no mind of its own except verbose condemnation. The war was carried on without let or hindrance till 1942. The Government could get all the men, all the money, and all the, material which their war efforts needed. Every Government loan was fully subscribed.

In 1942 came the Cripps Mission which presented to the Congress and to the rest of India Dead Sea Apple of useless promises, coupled as it was, with a clear hint of partition of India in the background. Naturally the Mission failed, but the Congress even while opposing the Mission's proposals yielded to the principle of partition after a very pretentious resolution reiterating its adherence to democracy and nationalism. At a meeting of the All India Congress Committee held in April 1942 at Allahabad the principle of partition was repudiated by an overwhelming majority – the minority consisting of the present

Governor General Mr. C. Rajagopalchari and his half dozen supporters-bent Maulana Azad, the so-called nationalist Muslim, who was then the President of the Congress. He gave a ruling a few months later that the Allahabad Resolution had no effect on the earlier resolution of the Working Committee which conceded the principle of Pakistan however remotely. The Congress was entirely at the end of its wits. The British Government went on effectively controlling the whole country through Muslim Ministries and through pro-Muslim Governors. The Princes wholly identified themselves with the war. Labor refused to keep aloof. The capitalist class supported the Congress in words and the Government in deed by supplying the Government everything it wanted at top prices. Even Khaddar enthusiasts sold blankets to Government. The Congress could see no way out of its absolute paralysis; it was out of office and Government was carried on in spite of its nominal opposition.

(k) 'Quit-India' by Congress and Divide and Quit' by League – Out of sheer desperation Gandhiji evolved the 'Quit India' Policy which was endorsed by the Congress. It was supposed to be the greatest national rebellion against foreign rule. Gandhiji had ordered the people to 'do or die'. But except that the leaders were quickly arrested and detained behind the prison bars some furtive acts of violence were practised by Congressmen for some weeks. But in less than three months the whole movement was throttled by Government with firmness and discretion. The movement soon collapsed. What remained was a series of piteous appeals by the Congress Press and the Congress supporters, who were outside the jail, for the release of the arrested leaders without formally withdrawing the 'Quit India' movement, which had already collapsed. Gandhiji even staged a fast to capacity for his release, but for two years until the Germans were decisively beaten, the leaders had to remain in jails and our Imperial masters were triumphant all along. Mr. Jinnah openly opposed the 'Quit India' Movement as hostile to the Muslims and raised a counter slogan 'Divide and Quit'. That is where Gandhiji's Hindu-Muslim Unity had arrived.

(1) Hindi Versus Hindustani – Absurdly pro-Muslim policy of Gandhiji is nowhere more blatantly illustrated than in his perverse attitude on the question of the National Language of India. By all the tests of a scientific language, Hindi has the most prior claim to be accepted as the National Language of this country. In the beginning of his career in India, Gandhiji gave, a great impetus to Hindi but as he found that the Muslims did not like it, he became a turncoat and blossomed forth as the champion of what is called, Hindustani. Everybody in India knows that there is no language called Hindustani; it has no grammar; it has no vocabulary; it is a mere dialect; it is spoken

but not written. It is a bastard tongue and a crossbreed between Hindi and Urdu and not even the Mahatma's sophistry could make it popular; but in his desire to please the Muslims he insisted that Hindustani alone should be the national language of India. His blind supporters of course blindly supported him and the so-called hybrid tongue began to be used. Words like 'Badshah Ram' and 'Begum Sita' were spoken and written but the Mahatma never dared to speak of Mr. Jinnah as Sri Jinnah and Maulana Azad as Pandit Azad. All his experiments were at the expense of the Hindus. His was a one-way traffic in his search of Hindu-Muslim Unity. The charm and the purity of the Hindi Language was to be prostituted to please the Muslims, but even Congressmen, apart from the rest of India refused to digest this nostrum. He continued to persist in his support to Hindustani The bulk of the Hindus however proved to be stronger and more loyal to their culture and to their mother tongue and refused to bow down to the Mahatmic fiat. The result was that Gandhiji did not prevail in the Hindi Parishad and had to resign from that body; his pernicious influence however remains and the Congress Governments in India still hesitate whether to select Hindi or Hindustani as the National Language of India. The barest common sense should make it clear to the meanest intelligence that the language of

80 per cent of the people must be the language of the country but his ostentatious support of the Muslims made him look almost idiotic when he continued to stand for Hindustani. Happily there are millions and millions of champions of the Hindi language and the Devnagari script. The U.P. Government has adopted Hindi as the language of the Province. The Committee appointed by the Government of India has translated the whole of the Draft Constitution in pure Hindi and it now remains for the Congress Party in the legislature to adopt the commensurable view in favor of Hindi or assert their loyalty to the Mahatma in their mad endeavor to force a foreign language on a great country like India. For practical purpose Hindustani is only Urdu under a different name, but Gandhiji could not have the courage to advocate the adoption of Urdu as against Hindi, hence the subterfuge to smuggle Urdu under the garb of Hindustani. Urdu is not banned by any nationalist Hindu but to smuggle it under the garb of Hindustani is a fraud and a crime. That is what the Mahatma tried to do. To bolster up a dialect in School Curriculum and in educational institutions that non-existent language in the garb of Hindustani because it pleased the Muslims was the communalism of the worst type on the part of the Mahatma. All these for Hindu-Muslim Unity.

(m) Vande Mataram Not to be Sung – The infatuation of Gandhiji for the Muslims and his incorrigible craving for Muslim leadership without any regard for right or wrong for truth or justice and in utter contempt of the sentiments of the Hindus as a whole was the high watermark of the Mahatmic benevolence. It is notorious that some Muslims disliked the celebrated song of 'Vande Mataram' and the Mahatma forthwith stopped its singing or recital wherever he could. This song has been honored for a century as the most inspiring exhortation to the Bengalees to stand up like one man for their nation. In the anti-partition agitation of 1905 in Bengal the song came to a special Prominence and popularity. The Bengalees swore by it and dedicated themselves to the Motherland at countless meetings where this song was sung. The British Administrator did not understand the true meaning of the song 'which simply meant 'Hail Motherland' Government therefore banned its singing forty years ago for some time, that only led to its increased popularity all over the country. It continued to be sung at all Congress and other national gatherings but as soon as one Muslim objected to it Gandhiji utterly disregarded the national sentiment behind it and persuaded the Congress also not to insist upon the singing as the national song. We are now asked to adopt Rabindranath Tagore's 'Jana Gana Mane, as a substitute for 'Vande Mataram'. Could anything be more demoralized or pitiful than this brazen-faced action against a song of world- wide fame? Simply because one ignorant fanatic disliked it. The right way to proceed would have been to enlighten the ignorant and remove the prejudice, but that is a policy which during the thirty years of unbounded popularity and leadership Gandhiji could not muster courage to try. His Hindu-Muslim Unity idea only meant to surrender, capitulate, and concede whatever the Muslims wanted. No wonder the willow-the-wisp unity never came and never could have come.

(n) Shiva Bavani Banned – Gandhiji banned the public recital or perusal of Shiva Bavani a beautiful collection of 52 verses by a Hindu poet in which he had extolled the great power of Shivaji and the protection which he brought to the Hindu community and the Hindu religion. The refrain of that collection says 'if there were no Shivaji, the entire country would have been converted to Islam.' (Here recite the couplet from the Book 'Shiva Bavani' ending with the words- (Kashiji Ki Kala jati Mathura masjid hoti Shivaji jo na hote to Sunnat hot Sabki)

This was the delight of millions of contemporary history and a beautiful piece of literature, but Gandhiji would have none of it. Hindu-Muslim Unity indeed!

(o) Suhrawardy Patronized – When the Muslim League refused to join the provisional Government which Lord Wavell invited Pandit Nehru to form; the League started a Council of Direct Action against any Government formed by Pandit Nehru, on the 15th of

August 1946. A little more than two weeks before Pandit Nehru was to take office, there broke out in Calcutta an open massacre of the Hindus which continued for three days unchecked. The horrors of these days are described in the 'Statesman' newspaper of Calcutta. At the time it was considered that the Government which could permit such outrages on its citizens must be thrown out; there were actual suggestions that Mr. Suhrawardy's Government should be dismissed, but the socialist Governor refused to take up the administration under Section 93 of the Government of India Act. Gandhiji however went to Calcutta and contracted a strange friendship with the author of these massacres; in fact he intervened on behalf of Suhrawardy and the Muslim League.

During the three days that the massacre of Hindus took place, the police in Calcutta did not interfere for the protection of life or property, innumerable outrages were practiced under the very eyes and nose of the guardians of law. but nothing mattered to Gandhiji.

To him Suhrawardy was an object of admiration from which he could not be diverted and publicly described Suhrawardy as a Martyr. No wonder two months later there was the most virulent outbreak of Muslim fanaticism in Noakhali and Tipperah 30,000 Hindu women were forcibly converted according to a report of Arya Samaj, the total number of Hindus killed or wounded was three lakhs not to say the crores of rupees worth of property looted and destroyed. Gandhiji then undertook, ostensibly alone, a tour of Noakhali District. It is well known that Suhrawardy gave him protection wherever he went and even with that protection Gandhiji never ventured to enter Noakhali District. All these outrages, loss of life and property were done when Surhawardy was the Prime Minister and to such a monster of inequity and communal poison Gandhiji gave the unsolicited title of Martyr.

(p) Attitude towards Hindu and Muslim Princes – Gandhiji's followers successfully humiliated the Jaipur, Bhavnagar and Rajkot States.

They enthusiastically supported even a rebellion in Kashmir State against the Hindu Prince. This attitude strangely enough contrasts with what Gandhiji did about the affairs in Muslim States. There was a Muslim League intrigue in Gwalior States, as a result of which the Maharaja was compelled to abandon the celebrations of the second millennium of the Vikram Calendar four years ago: the Muslim agitation was based on pure communalism The Maharaja is the liberal and impartial Ruler with a far-sighted outlook. In a recent casual Hindu Muslim clash in Gwalior because the Musalmans suffered some casualties Gandhiji came down upon the Maharaja with a vitriolic attack wholly undeserved.

(q) Gandhiji On Fast to Capacity – In 1943 while Gandhiji was on fast to capacity and nobody was allowed to interview him on political affairs, only the nearest and the dearest had the permission to go and enquire of his health. Mr. C. Rajagopalachari smuggled himself into Gandhiji's room and hatched a plot of conceding Pakistan which Gandhiji allowed him to negotiate with Jinnah. Gandhiji later on discussed this matter for three weeks with Mr. Jinnah in the later part of 1944 and offered Mr. Jinnah virtually what is now called Pakistan.

Gandhiji went every day to Mr. Jinnah's house, flattered him, praised him, embraced him, but Mr. Jinnah could not be cajoled out of his demand for the Pakistan pound of flesh. Hindu Muslim Unity was making progress in the negative direction.

(r) Desai-Liaquat Agreement – (i) In 1945 came the notorious Desai-Liaquat Agreement. It put one more, almost the last, nail in the coffin of the Congress as a National democratic body. Under that agreement, the late Mr. Bhulabhai Desai the then leader of the Congress party in the Central Legislative Assembly at Delhi entered into an agreement with Mr. Liaquat All Khan, the League Leader in the Assembly, jointly to demand a Conference from the British Government for the solution of the stalemate in Indian politics which was growing since the beginning of the War, Mr. Desai was understood to have taken that step without consulting anybody of any importance in the Congress circle, as almost all the Congress leaders had been detained since the 'Quit India' Resolution in 1942. Mr. Desai offered equal representation to the Muslims with Congress at the said Conference and this was the basis on which the Viceroy was approached to convene the Conference. The then Viceroy Lord Wavell flew to London on receipt of this joint request and brought back the consent of the Labor Government for the holding of the Conference. The official announcement in this behalf stupefied the country on account of its treachery alike to nationalism and democracy to which the Congress had become a party. Indian democracy was stabbed in the back and every principle of justice was violated. The Congress members quickly acquiesced in this monstrous proposal. The proposal however had, it was then revealed, the blessings of the Mahatma and was in fact made with his previous knowledge and consent. With the full agreement of the Congress party 25% of the people of India were, treated as if they were 50% and the 75% were brought down to the level of 50%. The Viceroy also laid down other conditions for the holding of the Conference. They were:

(1) An unqualified undertaking on the part of the Congress and all political parties to support the war against Japan until victory was won.

(2) A coalition Government would be formed in which the Congress and the Muslims would each

have five representatives. There will besides be a representative of the depressed classes, of the Sikhs and other Minorities.

(3) The Quit India Movement will be unconditionally withdrawn and such of the Congress leaders as had been detained in consequence of the Movement would be released.

(4) All measures of Administrative Reform will be within the four corners of the Government of India Act 1935.

(5) The Governor-General and the Viceroy shall retain the same constitutional position in the new setup as he had at that time i.e. he would remain the head of new Government.

(6) At the end of the war, the question of complete freedom will be decided through the machinery of the Constituent Assembly.

(7) If these were without any modification the Viceroy would reconstitute his Government with all portfolios to be held by Indians as per (2) above.

(8) People who had only three years ago started the 'Quit India' Movement for complete Independence and exhorted the people to 'Do or Die' in implementing the rebellion quietly submitted to accept office under the leadership of a British Viceroy on the terms, and conditions laid down by him, The fact was that the Quit India Movement

had failed, the Congress had no alternative program and events were moving on whether the Congress party was ready for them or not. Mr. Jinnah was the only gainer from the collapse of the Congress. He obtained a great tactical advantage by the recognition of the Muslims' right for 50% representation in all future discussions.

The two-nation theory and the demand for Pakistan received a fillip although the Conference failed without achieving the Hindu-Muslim Unity.

(s) Cabinet Mission Plant – Early in the year 1946 the so-called Cabinet mission arrived in India. It consisted of the then Secretary of State for India now Lord Lawrence, Mr. Alexander, the minister for War and Sir Stafford Cripps. Its arrival was heralded by a speech in Parliament by Mr. Atlee the prime Minister. Mr. Atlee announced in most eloquent terms the determination of the British Government to transfer power to India if only the latter agreed upon common plan.

The agreement was the pivot of the work of the mission but it was fatal. The Congress was honestly for a United India, but it was not outright in its conviction. It lacked firmness. Mr. Jinnah on the other hand demanded a divided India but he demanded it firmly. Between these two opposite demands the mission found it impossible to bring about an agreement and after some further informal discussions with both, the mission announced its own solution on the 15th May 1946.

It rejected and gave ten good reasons for that rejection but while firmly championing the unity of India the mission introduced Pakistan through the back door, In paragraph I5 of the proposals the mission introduced six conditions under which the British Government would be prepared to convene a Constituent Assembly invested with the right of framing a Constitution of Free India. Each of these six proposals were calculated to prevent the unity of India being maintained or full freedom being attained even if the Constituent Assembly was an elected body. The Congress party was so utterly exhausted by the failure of 'Quit India' that after some smoke-screen about its unflinching nationalism it virtually submitted to Pakistan by accepting the mission's proposals which made certain the dismemberment of India although in a roundabout manner. The Congress accepted the scheme but did not agree to form a Government. The long and short of it was that the Congress was called upon to form a Government and accept the whole scheme unconditionally. Mr. Jinnah denounced the British Government for treachery and started a direct action council of the Muslim League. The Bengal, the Punjab, the Bihar, the Bombay, and other places in various parts of India became scenes of bloodshed, arson, loot and rape on a scale unprecedented in history. The overwhelming members of victims were Hindus. The

Congress stood aghast but impotent and could not give any protection to the Hindus anywhere.

The Governor General in spite of his powers to intervene under the Act of 1935 in case of a breach of peace and tranquility in India or in any part of it merely looked on and made no use of his obligations under the Act. Few lakhs of people were killed, many thousands of women and children were kidnapped and few of them have not yet been traced, thousands and thousands of woman were raped, hundreds crores worth of property was looted, burned or destroyed.

The Mahatma was as far as ever before from his goal of Hindu-Muslim Unity.

(t) Congress Surrenders to Jinnah – By the following year the Congress Party abjectly surrendered to Mr. Jinnah at the point of bayonet and accepted Pakistan. What happened thereafter is too well-known. The thread running throughout this narrative is the increasing infatuation which Gandhiji developed for the Muslims. He uttered not one work of sympathy or comfort for millions of displaced Hindus, he had only one eye for humanity and that was the Muslim humanity. The Hindus simply did not count with him. I was shocked by all these manifestations of Gandhian saintliness.

(u) Ambiguous Statement about Pakistan – In one of his articles, Gandhiji while nominally ostensibly opposed to Pakistan, openly declared that if the Muslims wanted Pakistan at any cost, there was nothing to prevent them from achieving it. Only the Mahatma could understand what that declaration meant. Was it a prophesy or a declaration or disapproval of the demand for Pakistan?

(v) Ill-advice to Kashmir Maharaja – About Kashmir, Gandhiji again and again declared that Sheikh Abdullah should be entrusted the charge of the state and that the Maharaja of Kashmir should retire to Benares for no particular reason than that the Muslims formed the bulk of the Kashmir population. This also stands out in contrast with his attitude on Hyderabad where although the bulk of the Population is Hindu, Gandhiji never called upon the Nizam to retire to Mecca.

(w) Mountbatten vivisects India – From August 15, 1946 onwards the private armies of the Muslim League began killing, devastating and destroying the Hindus wherever they could lay their hands on. Lord Wavell, the then viceroy was undoubtedly greatly distressed at what was happening but he would not use his powers under the Government of India Act of 1935 to prevent such a holocaust and Hindu blood began to flow from Bengal to Karachi with mild reactions in the Deccan. All the time from the 2nd September 1946 the so-called National Government consisting of two hybrid elements utterly reconcilable to each other was in office but the Muslim League members who were 50% of the Congress did everything in their power to make the working of a Coalition Government impossible.

The Muslim League members did everything they could to sabotage the coalition Government but the more they became disloyal and treasonable to the Government of which they formed a part, the greater was Gandhiji's infatuation for them. Lord Wavell had to resign as he could not bring about a settlement. He had some conscience which prevented him from supporting the partition of India. He had openly declared it to be unnecessary and undesirable.

But his retirement was followed by the appointment of Mountbatten. King Log was followed by King Stork. This Supreme Commander of the South East Asia was a purely Military man and he had a great reputation for daring, and tenacity. He came to India with a determination to do or die and he 'did' namely he vivisected India.

He was more indifferent to human slaughter. Rivers of blood flowed under his very eyes and nose. He apparently was thinking that by the slaughter of Hindus so many opponents of his mission were killed, the greater the slaughter of the enemies greater the victory, and he pursued his aim relentlessly to its logical conclusion. Long before June 1948 the official date for handing over power, the wholesale murders of the Hindus had their full effect. The Congress which had boasted of its nationalism and democracy secretly accepted Pakistan literally at the point of the bayonet and abjectly surrendered to Mr. Jinnah. India was vivisected. One third of the Indian territory became foreign land to us from the 15th of August 1947. Lord Mountbatten came to be described in Congress Circle as the greatest Viceroy and Governor General India had ever known. He had gifted ten months earlier than 30th June 1948 what is called Dominion status to vivisected India. This is what Gandhiji had achieved after thirty years of undisputed dictatorship and this is what the Congress Party calls 'Freedom'. Never in the history of the world has such slaughter been officially connived at or the result described as Freedom, and 'Peaceful Transfer of power'. If what happened in India in 1946, 1947 and 1948 is to be called peaceful one wonders what would be the violent. Hindu Muslim Unity bubble was finally burst and a theocratic and communal State dissociated from everything that smacked of United India was established with the consent of Nehru and his crowd and they have called it 'Freedom won by them at sacrifice'. Whose sacrifice?

(x) Gandhiji on Cow slaughter – Gandhiji used to display a most vehement desire for the protection of the cow. But in fact he did no effort in that direction. On the contrary, in one of his post prayer speeches, he has admitted his inability to support the demand for stopping cow-slaughter. An extract from his speech in this connection is reproduced below.

Today Rajendra Babu informed me that he had received some fifty-thousand postcards, 20-30 thousand telegrams urging prohibition of cow-slaughter by law. In this connection I have spoken to you before also. After all why are so many letters and telegrams sent to me? They have not served any purpose. No law prohibiting cow-slaughter?

India can be enacted. How can I impose my will upon a person who does not wish voluntarily to abandon cow slaughter. India does not belong exclusively to the Hindus. Muslims, Parsees, Christians also live here. The claim of the Hindus that India has become the land of the Hindus is totally incorrect. This land belongs to all who live here.

I know an orthodox Vaishnava Hindu. He used to give beef soup to his child.

(y) Removal of Tricolor Flag – The tricolor flag with the Charkha on it was adopted by the Congress as the National Flag out of deference to Gandhiji. There were flag salutations on innumerable occasions. The flag was unfurled at every Congress meeting. It fluttered in hundreds at every session of National Congress; The Prabhat Pheries were never complete unless the flag was carried while the march was on. On the occasion of every imaginary or real success of the Congress Party, public buildings, shops and private residences were decorated with that flag. If any Hindu attached any importance to Shivaji's Hindu flag, "Bhagva Zenda" the flag which freed India from the Muslim-domination it was considered communal. Gandhiji's tri-coloured flag never protected any Hindu woman from outrage or a Hindu temple from desecration, yet the late Bhai Parmanand was once mobbed by enthusiastic Congressmen for not paying homage to that flag. University students showed their patriotism by mounting that flag on University building. A Mayor of Bombay is believed to have lost his Knighthood because his wife hoisted this flag on the Corporation building. Such was supposed to be the allegiance of the Congress people to their "National Flag". When the Mahatma was touring Noakhali and Tipperah in 1946 after the beastly outrages on the Hindus, the flag was flying on his temporary hut. But when a Muslim came there and objected to the presence of the flag on his head, Gandhiji quickly directed its removal. All the reverential sentiments of millions of Congressmen towards that flag were affronted in a minute, because that would please an isolated Muslim fanatic and yet the so-called Hindu-Muslim unity never took shape.

71. Some good number of people are laboring under the delusion that the freedom movement in India started with the advent of Gandhiji in 1914-15 and reached is consummation on the 15th August 1947 on which day it is said we attained Freedom under the leadership of the Father of the Nation. In all history there was never a more stupendous fiction fostered by the cunning and believed by the credulous in this country for over a thousand years. Far from attaining freedom under his leadership Gandhiji has left India torn and bleeding from a thousand wounds. There has been always alive in India a freedom

movement which has never been suppressed. When the Mahratta Empire was finally subdued in 1818 as the British thought the forces of freedom were lying low for some time in part of India but were actually challenging the supremacy of the British so far as Northern India was concerned through the rise of Sikh power.

And when by 1848 the Sikhs were defeated at Gujarat the rebelling of 1857 was being actively organised. It came with such suddenness and force and was so widespread that the British Imperialists began to shake in their shoes and more than once they seriously considered the advisability of leaving India. The history of the great effort on the part of the Indian people to overthrow the British yoke has been vividly described in the pages of Veer Savarkar's "War of Independence 1857" and by the time the British had fully regained control the Indian National Congress was established, once more to challenge the British domination and from 1885 the rational urge for freedom began to assert itself first through constitutional methods, later by militant methods. This fast developed into armed resistance which openly asserted itself through the bomb of Khudi Ram Bose in 1906.

72. Gandhiji arrived in India in 1914-15. Nearly eight years earlier, the revolutionary movement had spread over a large part of India.

The freedom Movement had never died out. It had risen again like the Phoenix from its ashes. After the arrival of Gandhiji and his fads of Truth and Non-violence, the movement began to suffer eclipse. Thanks however to Subhash Chandra Bose and the revolutionaries in Maharashtra, Punjab and Bengal that the movement continued to flourish parallel to Gandhiji's rise to leadership after the death of Lokamanya Tilak.

73. Even the constitutional movements carried on by the Moderates in the Congress registered some progress towards Freedom. In 1892 the British Government, were obliged to extend the then Legislative Councils. This was followed up by the Morley-Minto Reforms in 1909 when for the first time the elected representatives of the people secured the right to participate in the work of the Legislatures both by their voice and their votes. Twelve years thereafter later, after the first World War the Montague Chelmsford Reforms conceded partial Provincial Autonomy and also increased the number of elected members so as to give permanent non-official majority both at the Centre and in the Provinces; and in 1935, came the complete Provincial Autonomy and substantial Central responsibility which cover every subject except foreign policy, Army, and to some extent Finance. Gandhiji had no love for Parliamentary bodies. He called them prostitutes, and always urged their boycott. Yet the constitutional progress upto 1935, little though it was, had been achieved. The Act of 1935 was of course defective, more especially because of the numerous and vexation safeguards granted to the British vested interests and the premium it placed on communalism.

74. There was further objection to it on the ground of the veto which it granted to the Governors and the Governor General. Even then it is reasonably certain that if the Act had not been boycotted under Gandhiji's leadership, India would have long since reached the status of a Dominion which we are now supposed to be enjoying, after losing one-third of Indian territory.

75. I have already mentioned the revolutionary party which existed independent of the Congress. Amongst its sympathizers were many active Congressmen. This latter section was never reconciled to the yoke of Britain. During the First World War between 1914-1919 the Congress began to turn left and the terrorist movement outside was running parallel to the leftist party within. The Gadar Party was operating simultaneously in Europe and America in an effort to overthrow British Rule in India with the help of the Axis Powers. The 'Comagata Maru' incident is well known, and it is by no means clear that the "Emden" incident on the Madras beach was not due to the knowledge of the German Commander that India was seething with discontent. But from 1920 upwards Gandhiji discouraged, put his foot down on the use of force although he himself had carried on an active campaign for recruitment for soldiers of Britain only a few years earlier. The Rowlatt Report described at length the strength of the revolutionaries in India. Form 1906 till 1918 one Britisher after another and his Indian stooges were shot dead by the revolutionary nationalists and the British authorities were trembling about their very

existence. It was then that Mr. Montague came to this country as Secretary of State for India and promised the introduction of responsibility; even he was only partially successful to stern the tide of revolutionary fervor. The Government of India Act 1919 was over-shadowed by the Jallianwalla Bagh Tragedy in which hundreds of Indians were shot dead by General Dyer at a public meeting for the crime of holding a protest against the Rowlatt Act. Sir Michael O'Dwyer became notorious for callous and unscrupulous reprisals against those who had denounced the Rowlatt Act. Twenty years later he had to pay for it, when Udham Singh shot him dead in London. Chapekar brothers of Maharashtra, Pt. Shamji Krishna Verma the back bone of the Revolutionaries, Lala Hardayal, Virendranath Chatopadhyaya, Rash Behari Bose, Babu Arvind Ghosh, Khudiram Bose, Ulhaskar Datta, Madanlal Dhingra, Kanhere, Bhagatsingh, Rajguru, Sukhdeo, Chandrashekhar Azad were the living protest by Indian youth against the alien yoke. They had unfired and held aloft the flag of Independence, some of them long before Gandhiji's name was heard of and even when he was the accepted leader of the constitutional movement of the Indian National Congress.

76. I had already stated that the revolutionary movement beginning in Bengal and Maharashtra later on reached the Punjab. The young men associated with it did not come from the riffraff of society. They were educated, cultural men belonging to most respectable families having high social status in private life. They sacrificed

lives of comfort and ease at the altar of the liberty of the Motherland. They were the martyrs whose blood became the cementing force of Independence. Lokmanya Tilak built on it and the Mahatma got advantage of the accumulated momentum of this movement. It is my firm conviction that each stage of constitutional progress between 1909 and 1935 became possible as a result of the revolutionary forces working in the background.

77. Moderate's opinion condemned the revolutionary violence. Gandhiji publicly denounced it day after day on every platform and through the press. There is however little doubt that the overwhelming mass of the people gave their silent but wholehearted support to the vanguard of the armed resistance working for national freedom. The theory of the revolutionary is that a nation always tries to wage war on its alien conquerors. It owes no allegiance to the conqueror, and the very fact of his domination carries with it a notice to him that he may be overthrown any moment. The judgments passed on the armed resistance by a subject people to the foreign master, on the principle of allegiance of the citizen to his State is altogether beside the mark. And the more the Mahatma condemned the use of force in the country's battle for freedom the more popular it became. This fact was amply demonstrated at the Karachi Session of the Congress in March 1931; in the teeth of Gandhiji's opposition a resolution was passed in the open Session admiring the courage and the spirit of sacrifice of Bhagat Singh when he threw the bomb in

the Legislative Assembly in 1929. Gandhiji never forgot this defeat and when a few months later Mr. Hotson, the Acting Governor of Bombay was shot at by Gogate, Gandhiji returned to the charge at an All-India Congress Committee meeting and asserted that the admiration expressed by the Karachi Congress for Bhagat Singh was at the bottom of Gogate's action in shooting at Hotson. This astounding statement was challenged by Subhash Chandra Bose. He immediately came into disfavor with Gandhiji. To sum up, the share of revolutionary youth in the fight for Indian Freedom is by no means negligible and those who talk of India's freedom having been secured by Gandhiji are not only ungrateful but are trying to write false history. The true history of India from 1985 onwards for the freedom of the country will never be written so long as Indian affairs are in charge of the Gandhian Group. The memorable share of the youth will be kept back. It is nevertheless true that they have played a noble and creditable part.

78. It was not merely those who advocate the use of force in the freedom battle whom Gandhiji opposed. Even those who held political views radically different from his and those who did not accept his nostrums whom Gandhiji made the target of displeasure. An outrageous example of his dislike of people with whom he did not agree is furnished by the case of Subhash Chandra Bose. So far as I am aware no protest was ever made by Gandhiji against the deportation of Subhash for six years and Bose's election to the Presidential Chair of the Congress was

rendered possible only after he had personally disavowed any sympathy for violence. In actual practice however Subhash never toed the line that Gandhiji wanted during his term of office. And yet Subhash was so popular in the country that against the declared wishes of Gandhiji in favor of Dr. Pattabhi he was elected president of the Congress for a second time with a substantial majority even from the Andhra Desha, the province of Dr. Pattabhi himself. This upset Gandhiji beyond endurance and he expressed his anger in the Mahatmic manner full of concentrated venom by stating that the success of Subhash was his defeat and not that of Dr. Pattabhi. Even after this declaration, his anger against Subhash Bose was not gratified. Out of sheer cussedness he absented himself from the Tripuri Congress Session, staged a rival show at Rajkot by a wholly mischievous fast and not until Subhash was overthrown from the Congress Gaddi that the venom of Gandhiji became completely gutted.

79. This incident about the re-election of Subhash to the Congress crown and of his eventual expulsion from the Presidential office is an indication of the hypocrisy with which the Mahatma controlled and repudiated the Congress as and when he liked. He had repeatedly stated after 1934 with a great show of detachment that he was not even a four anna member of the Congress Party and that he had nothing to do with it. But when Subhash was elected for a second time Gandhiji complete lost his balance and furnished, the best proof that he had interfered with that election from the very inception

in favor of Dr. Pattabhi; it is a proof of his keen and engrossing interest in the rivalries and petty squabbles within the Congress at every stage while professing to be not even a member of that body.

80. When the 'Quit India' Movement was launched by the Congress on the 8th August 1942 in the initiative of Gandhiji most of its leaders were quickly arrested by Government before they could make any start and the movement so far as it was non-violent was nipped in the bud. There was another section in the Congress itself who went underground. These latter were not over-anxious to follow the Gandhian technique and to go to jail; on the contrary, they wanted to avoid going to jail as long as possible and in the meantime to do the maximum damage to Government by cutting communications, by,committing arson, loot and other acts of violence, not excluding murder. The statement of Gandhiji exhorting the people to 'Do or Die' was interpreted by that section as giving them full scope for all kinds of obstruction and sabotage. In fact they did everything to paralyze the war effort of Government to the fullest extent – Police thanas were burnt, postal communications were violently interrupted. In north Bihar and other places, nearly 900 railway stations were either burnt or destroyed and the administration was almost to a standstill for a time.

81. These activities were directly opposed to the Congress creed of non-violence and to the Satyagraha technique Gandhiji could neither support nor oppose these latter activities. If he supported them his creed of non-violence

would stand exposed. If he opposed them publicly he would become unpopular with the masses who did not care one brass button whether the expulsion of the British from India was accomplished by violence or non-violence. In fact, the Quit India campaign was known more for its acts of violence on the part of Congress supporters than for anything else. Gandhiji's non-violence had died within few weeks of the starting the 'Quit India' campaign while the violence that was being committed under that flame found no favor with him. The Gandhian point of view was entirely absent from the activities of the Congress party and its supporters within a few weeks of the 8th August 1942. No where was non-violence either preached or practiced as the supporters of the campaign were, in the words of Gandhiji himself, prepared to 'Do or Die'. It was only when Lord Linlithgow in his correspondence with Gandhiji in 1943 categorically challenged him to own or disown the violence on the part of the supporters of the 'Quit India' campaign that Gandhiji was forced to condemn that violence. Whatever embarrassment, damage, inconvenience and harm were done to the war efforts was the result of the violent activities of the Congress supporters and not the so-called non-violence of the Mahatma. Non-violence had completely failed; violence to some extent appeared to have succeeded, but Gandhiji had to denounce it from the jail. The revolutionary struggle for independence was thus discouraged by Gandhi while his own strategy had completely collapsed soon after the 8th August 1942.

82. By this time Mr. Subhash Chandra Bose who had mysteriously escaped from India early in January 1941 had already arrived in Japan after reaching Berlin through Afghanistan. The way in which Mr. Subhash Chandra Bose escaped from Calcutta in January 1941 and the hardships and sufferings which he had to undergo on his way through the Indian Frontier to Kabul and thence after to Berlin are vividly described by Mr. Uttam Chand in his book 'When Bose was Ziauddin'. The courage and tenacity with which Bose faced all privations, all dangers, all difficulties, eventually reaching Berlin made the most thrilling and romantic reading. By the time of the arrival of the Cripps Mission in India in 1942 he had already reached Japan and was organizing an invasion of India. Before Subhash left Germany, Hitler had invested him with the title of His Excellency and on reaching Japan he found the Japanese ready to assist him against the British in the invasion of the country. Japan had already joined the war on the side of the axis by the attack on the Pearl Harbor in America; Germany had declared war on Russia; and Britain, France in turn had declared war on Italy and Germany and Japan. In Japan in Federated Malaya States, in Burma and its other parts of the Far East, Subhash received most enthusiastic welcome and immense support from the Indians settled there.

83. The Japanese had intensified their war effort and occupied Burma, Dutch East Indies, Federated Malaya States and the whole of the Far East including the Andaman Islands. Subhash Chandra Bose was thereby enabled to start a

provisional Indian Republican Government on Indian territory. By 1944 he was equipped to start on an invasion of India with the help of the Japanese. Pandit Nehru had declared that, if Subhash Chandra Bose came into India with the support of the Japanese he would fight Subhash. Early in 1944, Japanese and the Indian National Army organised by Subhash were thundering at the gates of India and they had already entered Manipur State and some part of the Assam Frontier. The I. N. A. consisted of volunteers from the Indian population of the Far East and of those Indians who had deserted to the I. N. A. from the Japanese prisons. That the campaign eventually failed was no fault of Subhash; his men fought like the Trojans. But his difficulties were far too great and his army was not sufficiently equipped with modern armaments. The I.N.A. had no airplanes and their supply-line was weak, many died of starvation and illness as there was no adequate medical treatment available to them. But the spirit which Subhash engendered in them was wonderful. He was lovingly described by them as Netaji Subhash Chandra Bose, and they had adopted the slogan of 'Jai Hind' under his leadership.

84. Gandhiji was opposed to Subhash Chandra Bose's invasion of India. Nehru was opposed to him because he did not approve of Bose's support to the Japanese invader. But whatever difference may have existed between Bose and other Indian leaders there was no doubt whatever that Subhash was loved more than any other leader because of his singlehanded effort to destroy British imperialism.

If Subhash had been alive and had entered India in 1945 after the defeat of the Japanese army, the whole Indian population would, like one man, have been behind him and given him the most affectionate welcome, But Gandhiji was again luckier. Lokmanya Tilak died in 1920 and Gandhiji became the unchallenged leader. Success of Subhash Chandra would have a crushing defeat for Gandhiji, but luck was again on his side and Subhash Chandra died outside India. It then became easy for the Congress party to profess love and admiration for Subhash Chandra Bose and the I. N. A. and even to defend some of its officers and men in the Great State Trial in 1946. They even adopted 'Jai Hind' as the slogan which Subhash had introduced in the East. They traded on the name of Subhash and the I. N. A. and the two issues which led them to victory during the election in 1945-46 were their hypocritical homage to Subhash's memory, moreover the Congress party had promised they were opposed to Pakistan and would resist it at all costs. On these two assurances they treated the I.N.A. with scant courtesy and of course they succumbed to Pakistan in breach of their promise.

85. All this time the Muslim League was carrying on treasonable activities, disturbing the peace and tranquility of India carrying on a murderous campaign against the Hindus. Lord Wavell and Lord Mountbatten looked on entirely unconcerned. The Congress would not venture to condemn or to stop these wholesale massacres in pursuit of its policy of appeasement at all costs. Gandhiji suppressed everything which did not fit in with his pattern

of public activities. I am therefore surprised when claims are made over and again the winning of the freedom was due to Gandhiji. My own view is that constant pandering of the Muslim League was not the way to winning freedom. It only created a Frankenstein which ultimately devoured its own creator swallowing one third of hostile, sensoriour, unfriendly and aggressive Indian territory, and permanently stationing a neighbor on what was once Indian territory. About the winning of Swaraj and freedom, I maintain the Mahatma's contribution was negligible. But I am prepared to give him a place as a sincere patriot. His teachings however have produced opposite result and his leadership has stultified the nation. In my opinion S. C. Bose is the supreme hero and martyr of modern India. He kept alive and fostered the revolutionary mentality of the masses, advocating all honorable means, including the use of force when necessary for the liberation of India. Gandhiji and his crowd of self-seekers tried to destroy him. It is thus entirely incorrect to represent the Mahatma as the architect of Indian Independence.

86. The real cause of the British leaving this country is threefold and it does not include the Gandhian method. The aforesaid triple forces are:

(i) The movements of the Indian Revolutionaries right from 1857 to 1932, i.e. up to the death of Chandra Shekhar Azad at Allahabad, then next, the movement of revolutionary character not that of Gandhian type in the countrywide rebellion of 1942 and an armed revolt put up by Subhash Chandra Boss the result of which was a spread of the revolutionary mentality in the Military Forces of India are the real dynamic factors that have shattered the very foundations of the British Rule in India. And all these effective, efforts to freedom were opposed by Gandhiji.

(ii) So also a good deal of credit must be given to, those who, imbibed with a spirit of patriotism, fought with the Britishers strictly on constitutional lines on the Assembly floors and made a notable progress in Indian politics. The view of this section was to take the maximum advantage of whatever we have obtained and to fight further on. This section was generally represented by late Lokmanya Tilak, Mr. N. C. Kelkar, Mr. C. R. Das, Mr. Vithhalbhai Patel, brother of Hon. Sardar Patel, Pandit Malaviya, and Bhai Parmanand and during last ten years by prominent Hindu Sabha leaders. But this school of men of sacrifices and intelligence was also ridiculed by Gandhiji himself and, his followers by calling them as job hunters or power seekers, although they often ultimately resorted to the same methods.

(iii) There is also one more but nonetheless important reason for the Britishers which made them part with power and that is the advent of Labor Government and an overthrow of Mr. Churchill, superimposed by the frightful economic conditions and the financial bankruptcy to which the war had reduced Britain.

87. So long as Gandhian method was in ascendance, frustration was the only inevitable result. He had throughout opposed every spirited revolutionary, radical and vigorous individual or group, and constantly boosted his Charkha, non-violence and truth. The Charkha after 34 years of the best efforts of Gandhiji, had only led to the expansion of the machine-run textile industry by over 200 per cent. It is unable even now to clothe even one per cent of the nation. As regards non-violence, it was absurd to expect 40 crores of people to regulate their lives on such a lofty plane and it broke down most conspicuously in 1942. As regards truth the least I can say is that the truthfulness of the average Congressman is by no means of a higher order than that of the man in the street and that very often it is untruth in reality masked by a thin veneer of pretended truthfulness.

88. Really speaking the idea of Hindu-Muslim Unity which Gandhiji had put forward when he entered Indian Politics, came to an end from the moment Pakistan was established, because the Muslim league was opposed to regard India as one whole nation; and over and over again they had stated with great obstinacy, that they were not Indians. The Hindu-Muslim Unity which Gandhiji himself had put forward many a time was not of this type. What he wanted was that they both should take part in the struggle for independence as comrades. That was his idea of Hindu-Muslim Unity. The Hindus followed Gandhiji's advice but the Muslims on every occasion disregarded it and indulged in such behavior as would be insulting to the

Hindus, and at last, it has culminated in the vivisection and division of the country.

89. The mutual relations of Gandhiji and Mr. Jinnah are also worthy to note. When Mr. Jinnah who was once an ardent nationalist became rank communalist from 1920 and onward, since then he put forward one evident and clear fact that it was his intention to look to the interests of the Muslim community and that the Muslims should not at all rely upon the Congress and the Congress leaders; and that the Muslims should not support the fight for freedom along with the Congress. Mr. Jinnah had also openly demanded Pakistan. He has preached these doctrines quite openly. He deceived no one as far as principles are concerned. His was the behavior of an open enemy. He could talk of vivisecting this country with ease and wholly unfettered tongue.

90. Gandhiji had seen Mr. Jinnah many a time and called upon him. Every time he had to plead to him as "Brother Jinnah." He even offered to him the Premiership of the whole of India; but there was not a single occasion on which Mr. Jinnah had shown any inclination even to co-operate.

91. Gandhiji's inner voice, his spiritual power and his doctrine of non-violence of which so much is made of, all crumbled before Mr. Jinnah's iron will and proved to be powerless.

92. Having known that with his spiritual powers he could not influence Mr. Jinnah, Gandhiji should have either changed his policy or should have admitted his defeat and

given way to others of different political views to deal with Mr. Jinnah and the Muslim League. But Gandhiji was not honest enough to do that. He could not forget his egoism or self even for national interest. There was, thus, no scope left for the practical politics while the great blunders as big as the Himalayas were being committed.

93. Constantly for nearly one year after the horrible Noakhali massacre, our nation was as if bathing in the pool of blood. The Muslims indulged in horrible and dreadful massacre of humanity followed by reactions from Hindus in some parts. The attacks of Hindus on Muslims in the East Punjab, Bihar or Delhi, were simply acts of reaction. It is not that Gandhiji did not know that the basic cause of these reactions was the outrages on Hindus by the Muslims in the Muslim majority Provinces. But still Gandhiji went on condemning strongly such actions of Hindus only, and the Congress Government went to the extent of threatening to even bombard the Hindus in Bihar to check their discontent and reactions against Muslims which was mainly due to the Muslim outbursts and atrocities in Noakhali and elsewhere. Gandhiji had often advocated during the course of his prayers that the Hindus in India should treat the Muslims with respect and generosity even though the Hindus and Sikhs in Pakistan may be completely massacred, and though Mr. Suhrawardy may be the leader of the Goondas, he should be allowed to move about freely and safely in Delhi. This will be evident from extracts given below from Gandhiji's post-prayer speeches:

(a) "We should with a cool mind reflect when we are being swept away. Hindus should never be angry against the Muslims even if the latter might make up their minds to undo even their existence. If they put all of us to the sword, we should court death bravely, may they, even rule the world, we, shall inhabit the world. At least we should never fear death. We are destined to be born and die; then why need we feel gloomy over it? If all of us die with a smile on our lips, we shall enter a new life. We shall originate a new Hindustan." (6th April 1947).

(b) "The few gentlemen from Rawalpindi who coiled upon me today were sturdy, brave and absorbed in business. I advised them to remain calm. After all God is great. There is no place where God does not exist, meditate on Him and take His name; everything will be all right. They asked me what about those who still remain in Pakistan. I asked them why all they came here (in Delhi). Why they did not die there? I still hold on to the belief one should stick to the place where we happen to live even if we are cruelly treated and even killed. Let us die if the people kill us; but we should die bravely with the name of God on our tongue. Even if our men are killed, why should we feel angry with anybody, you should realize that even if they are killed they have had a good and proper end. May the heaven make us all so.

May God send us the same way. This is what we should pray heartily for. I will advise you (and issue) as I did to the residents of Rawalpindi, that they should go there and meet the Sikhs and Hindu refugees, tell them politely to return to their places in Pakistan unaided either by Police or the Military." (23rd September 1947).

(c) "Not one of those who have died in Punjab is going to return. In the end we too have to go there. It is true that they were murdered but then some others die of cholera or due to other causes. He who is born must die. If those killed have died bravely, they have not lost anything but earned something. But what to do with those who have slaughtered people is a big question. One may concede that to err is human. A human being is a bundle of errors. In Punjab our protection is due to them (British troops). But is this protection? I want even if a handful of persons should protect themselves. They should not be afraid of death. After all the killers will be none other than our Muslim brothers. Will our brothers cease to be our brothers after change of their religion? And do we not act like them? What thing we left undone with women in Bihar."

94. Gandhiji needs have taken into consideration that the desire for reprisals springing tip in the Hindu mind was simply a natural reaction. Thousands of Hindus in the Muslim Provinces were being massacred simply because

of the fault of their being Hindus, and our Government was quite unable to render these unfortunate people any help or protection. Could it be in any way unnatural if the waves of sorrow and grief of the Hindus in those Provinces should redound on the mind and hearts of the Hindus in other Provinces? It was not at all unnatural, for these reactions wore only the signs of warm humanity. Only with the sole object of redressing the woes and calamities of their fellow brothers in those provinces and giving them protection, that the retaliation against the Muslim was resorted to, as the Hindus believed that was the only way by which the atrocities of the Muslims could be checked. When the people (Hindus) noticed and realized that the Indian Union Government was unable to afford any protection to their brethren residing in Pakistan, they thought of taking the law in their own hands. The retaliatory actions taken by the Hindus in Bihar and elsewhere were the inevitable outcome of the revulsion left by the Hindus at the shocking atrocities in other provinces. Such a feeling at times also is as spiritual and natural as that of kindness.

95. Many a great revolution has been successful only by the idea of this sort of feeling of acute discontent against the misdeeds of the rulers. It would be quite impossible to put an end to the governance of the Society by the wicked, had it not been for such feelings of discontent, retaliation and revenge springing up against the wicked Dictators. The events of ancient history as depicted in Ramayana and Mahabharat, or the more modern wars of England

and America against Germany and Japan too indicate the some sort of action and reaction. It may be either good or bad. Such is the human nature.

96. Looked at from the point of view of the Indian politics, I have already shown in my narration elsewhere, how Gandhiji had strongly opposed several efforts made for winning the freedom of the country. There was no consistency in his political policy; in particular his behavior at the time of the last war was quite unthinkable.

97. He first gave out the principle that no help should be given by India to the war between England and Germany. "WAR MEANT VIOLENCE AND HOW COULD I HELP" was his saying. But the wealthy companions and followers of Gandhiji enormously added to their wealth by undertaking contracts from the Government for the supply of materials for war. It is needless for me to mention names but all know the wealthy personalities like Birla, Dalmia, Walchand Hirachand, Nanjibhai Kalidas, etc. Gandhiji and his Congress colleagues have been much helped by every one of them. But Gandhiji never refused to accept the monies offered by these wealthy people although it was got from this blood-filled war. Nor did he prevent these wealthy people from carrying out their contracts with the Government for the supply of materials for war. Not only that but Gandhiji had given his consent to taking up the contract for supplying blankets to the army from the Congress Khadi Bhandar.

98. Gandhiji's release from jail in 1944 was followed by the release of other leaders also, but the Government had to be assured by the Congress leaders of their help in the war against Japan. Gandhiji not only did not oppose this but actually supported the Government proposal.

99. In Gandhiji's politics there was no place for consistency of ideas and reasons. Truth was what Gandhiji only could define. His politics was supported by old superstitious belief such as the power of the soul, the inner voice, the fast, the prayer, and the purity of mind.

100. Gandhiji had once said, 'FREEDOM GOT FROM NON-VIOLENCE A THOUSAND YEARS LATER IS PREFERABLE TO THE FREEDOM GOT TO-DAY BY VIOLENCE.' Whether he acted as he said, or whether his actions and sayings were diametrically opposed to each other can be inferred to some extent from the example cited above.

101. A recent example of the inconsistency of his doctrine of nonviolence is worth being noted in particular. The problem of Kashmir followed very closely that of Pakistan. Pakistan had begun a dreadful invasion to conquer and gulp down the Kashmir. H.H. the Maharaja of Kashmir had asked for help from the Nehru Government, and the latter in return agreed to do so on condition that Sheikh Abdullah would be made the Chief Administrator. On every important matter Pt. Nehru had consulted Gandhiji. There was every chance of partiality being done, Kashmir being the birth-place of Pt. Nehru. And to give no way

to this partiality, Pt. Nehru consulted Gandhiji about sending Military help to Kashmir and it was only on the consent of Gandhiji that Pt. Nehru sent troops for the protection and defense of Kashmir. Pt. Nehru himself has told this in one of his speeches.

102. Our political leaders knew from the very beginning that the invasion of Kashmir by the raiders was supported by Pakistan. And it was therefore, evident that sending help to the Kashmir meant waging war directly against Pakistan. Gandhiji himself was opposed to the war with arms, and he has told this to the entire world again and again. But he gave his consent to Pt Nehru to send army in Kashmir. The only conclusion that could be drawn from what is happening in Kashmir is that, today after the attainment of freedom for the partitioned India, that under Gandhiji's blessings, our Government has resorted to the war where man-killing machinery is being used.

103. Had Gandhiji a firm belief in the doctrine of non-violence, he should have made a suggestion for sending Satyagrahis instead of the armed troops and tried the experiment. Orders should have been issued to send 'Takalis' in place of rifles and 'Spinning wheels' (i.e. Charkhas) instead of the guns. It was a golden opportunity for Gandhiji to show the power of his Satyagraha by following his precept as an experiment at the beginning of our freedom.

104. But Gandhiji did nothing of the sort. He had begun a new war by his own will, at the very beginning of the existence of Free India. What does this inconsistency

mean? Why did Gandhiji himself so violently trample down the doctrines of non-violence, he had championed? To my mind, the reason for his doing so is quite obvious; and it is that this war is being fought for Sheikh Abdullah. The administrative power of Kashmir was going in the hands of Muslims and for this reason and this reason alone did Gandhiji consent to the destruction of the raiders by Armed Forces. Gandhiji was reading the dreadful news of Kashmir war, while at the same time fasting to death only because a few Muslims could not live safely in Delhi. But he was not bold enough to go on fast in front of the raiders of Kashmir, nor had he the courage to practice Satyagraha against them. All his fasts were to coerce Hindus.

105. I thought it rather a very unfortunate thing that in the present 20th Century such a hypocrite should have been regarded as the leader of the All-India politics. The mind of this Mahatma was not affected by the attacks on the Hindus in Hyderabad State; and this Mahatma never asked the Nizam of Hyderabad to abandon his throne. If the Indian politics proceeded in this way under the guiding dominance of Gandhiji, even the preservation of freedom obtained today – even though in partitioned India would be impossible. These thoughts arose in my mind again and again and it was full with them. As the above incidents were taking place, Gandhiji's fast for the Hindu-Muslim Unity was announced on 13th January 1948, and then I lost nearly my control on my feelings.

106. For the fast four years, I had been working as the Editor

of a daily newspaper, and even before this period, I have spent most of my time in the service of the public. As such therefore I was in a habit of being in touch with all the Indian political developments.

107. I was fully aware of the idea of the mutual relations among the three political bodies – the Muslim League, the Congress and the Hindu Mahasabha. The Muslim League had always dubbed the Congress as a Hindu organization but the Congress leaders were ashamed of being called a Hindu body. The Congressmen felt abused when called 'Communal.'

108. Really speaking, if any institution were to look to the interests of a particular community without hindering the growth of national spirit, why should one use the word 'Communal' in the sense of an abuse to that institution? It would be proper if an institution seeking the interests of any particular community by destroying the very essence of the national spirit were to be abused as being a selfish 'Communal-minded' body. But the Congress has no such discretion.

The Congress has styled both the Muslim League and the Hindu Mahasabha as 'Communal' bodies using the word 'Communal' as an expression of abuse. But the thing to be specially noted is that while the Congress has yielded to every demand of the Muslim League it has not taken due notice of even the purely national policy of the Hindu Mahasabha and has carried on propaganda of distortion against Hindu Mahasabha and its leaders.

109. When the Congress recognized the Muslim League as representing the- Muslim Community, viewed from logical point of view it would not have been out of place to recognize the Hindu Mahasabha as representing the Hindus, or at least the Congress should openly have declared that it would look to the interests of the Hindus. But the Congress never did that. As a result of all this in spite of the existence of a very powerful body such as the Muslim League looking after the interests of the Muslims, a few Muslims who were still the members of the Congress also looked after the Muslim interest, whereas there was none to look after the Hindu interest as such. But the Congress which decided the Hindu Mahasabha by calling it 'Communal' took part in the conference of leaders convened by H. E. Lord Wavell at Simla and accepted the principle of 50 percent, representation of the Muslims. Not only that, but at the instance of Gandhiji the Congress leaders were prepared to be recognized as representatives of Caste Hindus. This position taken by the Congress was the most hideously communal one being entirely the outcome of the Muslim-appeasing policy adopted by it.

110. Was this the ideal of freedom and, independence of India, torn by vivisection, before the Congress, after the foundation of which our great national, intelligent and sacrificing leaders labored assiduously by keeping before them the ideal of the freedom of the whole nation, sacrificed even their lives for their ideal of the achievement of complete democracy, and tried for the mutual co-

operation among the major and minor communities of this vast country and in the freedom fight of which the parts of the Punjab, the Bengal, the Sind, and the N. W. F. Province, which now form the Pakistan, were in no way less prominent than any other part of India? So also, could those patriots with their ideal of the freedom of the whole of Bharatkhand, who were, though outside the Congress, in the forefront of the revolutionists who either gladly went to the gallows or passed their days out of their motherland as exiles, or were rotting in the dark cells of the Andamans dream of freedom as envisaged in the freedom granted to the country by vivisection? It is but proper that the award for their incomparable sacrifices should be in the establishment of a State founded upon blind and fanatic religious faith in one part of the country?

111. But the Congress under the leadership of Gandhiji commenced its surrender to the Muslims, right from the time the 14 demands of Mr. Jinnah were made till the establishment of the Pakistan. Is it not a deplorable sight for people to see the Congress celebrate the occasion of the establishment of a Dominions Government in the rest of country shattered and vivisected by the Pakistan in the East and West and 'with the pricking thorn of Hyderabad in its midst. On seeing this downfall of the Congress under the dominance of Gandhiji, I am reminded of the well known verse of Raja Bhartrihari to the effect:

(The Ganges has fallen from the Heavens on the head of Shiva, thence on the Himalayas, thence on the earth, and thence in the sea. In this manner, down and down she went and reached a very low stage.

Truly it is said that indiscriminate persons deteriorate to the low position in a hundred ways).

112. The day on which I decided to remove Gandhiji from the political stage it was clear to me that personally I shall be lost to everything that could be mine. I am not a moneyed person but I did have a place of honor and respect amongst those known as middle class society. I have been in the public life of my Province and the service that I have been able to render so far has given me a place of honor and respect amongst my people. Ideas of culture and civilization are not strange to me. I had in my view before me some scheme of constructive work to be taken in hand in my future life and I felt I had enough strength and enthusiasm to undertake them and carry them out successfully. I have maintained robust, health and I do not suffer from any bodily defect and I am not addicted to any vice.

Although I myself am not a much-learned man, I have a great regard and admiration for the learned.

113. Since the year 1929-30 when the Congress launched its first campaign of the Civil Disobedience Movement, I entered the life of a public worker. I was merely a student then, but the lectures relating to this movement and the accounts thereof published in the newspapers had greatly impressed me and I resolved to join the movement and take the career of a public worker. Just

after when this movement was over the problems relating to Muslims assumed grave appearance and a movement to bring about the unification of the Hindus was being taken in hand more intensely by the Hindu Sabha leaders like Dr. Moonje, Bhai Parmanandji, Pandit Madan Mohan Malaviya as also by some leaders of the Arya Samaj and by the workers of the Rashtriya Swayam Sevak Sangh. The question of Communal Award was under hot discussion amongst all the political bodies and it is also noteworthy to mention here that in the Session of the Hindu Mahasabha which was held at Poona in the year 1935, it was decided to contest the elections for legislatures against the Congress as the views of the latter were unfairly in favor of the Muslims and detrimental to the Hindus. This contest against the Congress was decided by the Hindu Mahasabha under the auspices of the late Pandit Madan Mohan Malaviya who was also a veteran leader of the Congress.

114. About the year 1932 late Dr. Hedgewar of Nagpur founded the Rashtriya Swayam Sevak Sangh in Maharashtra also. His oration greatly impressed me and I joined the Sangh as a volunteer there of. I am one of those volunteers of Maharashtra who joined the Sangh in its initial stage. I also worked for a few years on the intellectual side in the Province of Maharashtra. Having worked for the uplift of the Hindus I felt it necessary to take part in the political activities of the country for the protection of the just rights of Hindus. I therefore left the Sangh and joined the Hindu Mahasabha.

115. In the year 1938, I led the first batch of volunteers who marched into the territory of the. Hyderabad State when the passive resistance movement was started by the Hindu Mahasabha, with a demand for Responsible Government in the State. I was arrested and sentenced to one year's imprisonment. I have personal experience of the uncivilized, nay barbarous rule of Hyderabad, and have undergone corporal punishment of dozens of cane slashes, for the offence of singing the 'Vande Mataram' song at the time of prayer.

116. In the year 1943 the Bihar Government had issued a proclamation prohibiting the holding of the Hindu Mahasabha Session at Bhagalpur. The Mahasabha resolved to defy this ban as it felt that the action of the Government was unjust and illegal. The session was held in spite of all the precautions taken by the Government for its prevention. I took a leading part in the preparation for the session keeping myself underground for nearly a month. During this period while reading newspapers I have come across items of news appreciating my work I have also heard people expressing their approval of my part in public life. By nature I am not a person of violent temperament. The approver Badge in his deposition at Page 225 has stated that I took out a knife to stab Mr. Bhopatkar. This statement it totally false. Mr. Bhopatkar is at present leading the lawyers defending the accused. Had I made any such assault as described by the approver could he have come forward to render us assistance in

our defense? If that alleged incident were true, I should have least thought of taking the help of Mr. Bhopatkar.

117. Those, who personally know me, take me as a person of quiet temperament. But when the top rank leaders of the Congress with the consent of Gandhiji divided and tore the country which we consider as a deity of worship my mind became full with the thoughts of direful anger.

I wish to make it clear that I am not an enemy of the Congress. I have always regarded that body as the premier institution which has worked for the political uplift of the country. I had and have my differences with its leaders. This will be clearly seen from my letter addressed to Veer Savarkar on 28th February 1933 (RX D/30) which is in my hand and signed by me and I admit its contents.

118. There was no enmity between Gandhiji and myself on any personal grounds. To those who speak of Gandhiji's honest motive in supporting Pakistan, I have only to say that I had nothing but the purest interest of our nation at my heart in taking the extreme step against the person of Gandhiji, who was the most responsible and answerable person for the terrible event culminating in the creation of Pakistan. I could foresee the result of my action against the life of Gandhiji and did very well realize that the moment the people come to know about it they would change their view about me in spite of the circumstances. My status and honor in the society and the sympathies which the people entertained for me will be smashed completely. I fully realized that I would be looked upon as the most despicable fellow in the society.

119. I had a very good idea about fiery attacks that would be launched against me in the Press. But I never thought that I could be cowed down by the fire poured against me by the Press. For, had the Indian Press impartially criticized the anti-national policy carried on by Gandhiji and had they impressed upon the people that the interest of the nation was far greater than the whim of any individual howsoever great he may be, Gandhiji and his followers could never have dared concede Pakistan to the Muslims as easily as has been done. The Press had displayed such weakness and submission to the High Command of the Congress that it allowed the mistakes of leaders pass away freely and unnoticed and made vivisection easy by their policy. The fear about such Press – weak and subservient as it was – could not therefore dislodge me from my resolve.

120. It is stated in some quarters that the people could not have got the independence unless Pakistan was conceded. But I took it to be an utterly incorrect and untrue view. To me it appears to be merely a poor excuse to justify the action taken by the leaders. The leaders of the Gandhian creed often claim to have conquered ' Swarajya' by their struggle. If they had conquered Swarajya, then it would be clearly seen that it is most ridiculous to say that those Britishers who yielded, were in a position to lay down the condition of Pakistan before the grant of independence could be only one reason for Gandhiji and his followers to give their consent to the creation of Pakistan and it is that these people were accustomed to make a show of

hesitation and resistance in the beginning and ultimately to surrender to the Muslim demands.

121. Pakistan was conceded on the 15th of August 1947, and how? Pakistan was conceded by deceiving the people and without any consideration for the feelings and opinions of the people of Punjab, Bengal N.W.F. Province, Sind, etc. Indivisible Bharat was divided into two and in one of its parts a theocratic State was established. The Muslims obtained the fruit of their anti-national movements and actions in the shape of Pakistan. The leaders of the Gandhian creed ridiculed the opponents of Pakistan as traitors and communal minded, while they themselves helped in the establishment of a Muslim State in India yielding to the demands of Mr. Jinnah. This event of Pakistan had upset the tranquility of my mind. But even after the establishment of Pakistan if this Gandhian Government had taken any steps to protect the interests of Hindus in Pakistan it could have been possible for me to control my mind which was terribly shaken on account of this terrible deception of the people. But, after handing over crores of Hindus to the mercy of the Muslims of Pakistan Gandhiji and his followers have been advising them not to leave Pakistan but continue to stay on. The Hindus thus were caught in the hands of Muslim authorities quite unawares and in such circumstances series of calamities followed one after the other. When I bring to my mind all these happenings my body simply feels a horror of burning fire, even now.

122. Every day that dawned brought forth the news about thousands of Hindus being massacred, Sikhs numbering 15000 having been shot dead, hundreds of women torn of their clothes being made naked and taken into procession and that Hindu women were being sold in the market places like cattle. Thousands and thousands of Hindus had to run away for their lives and they had lost everything of theirs. A long line of refugees extending over the length of 40 miles was moving towards the Indian Union. How was this terrible happening counter-acted by the Union Government? Oh! by throwing bread to the refugees from the air.

123. These atrocities and the blood-bath would have to some extent been checked if the Indian Government had lodged strong protests against the treatment meted out to the Minorities in Pakistan or even if a cold threat had been held out to the Muslims in India of being treated in the same manner as a measure of retaliation. But the Government which was under the thumb of Gandhiji resorted to absolutely different ways. If the grievances of the minorities in Pakistan were voiced in the Press, it was dubbed as an attempt to spread disaffection amongst the communities and made an offence and the Congress Governments in several Provinces started demanding securities under the Press Emergency Powers Act, one after the other. I was alone served with notices demanding securities to the extent of Rs. 16,000 and in the Bombay Province alone nearly 900 such cases have occurred, as is stated by the Home Member, Mr. Morarjibhai Desai in

the Court. Nothing was done to redress the grievances of the Press even though Press deputations waited upon the Ministers. Thus there was total disappointment in my attempt to bring pressure by peaceful means upon the Congress Governments guided by Gandhian creed.

124. When all these happenings were taking place in Pakistan, Gandhiji did not even by a single word protest and censure the Pakistan Government or the Muslims concerned. The Muslim atrocities resorted to in Pakistan to root out the Hindu culture and the Hindu society have been entirely due to the teachings of Gandhiji and his behavior. If the Indian politics had been handled in a practical manner there would never have been the terrible human slaughter as has taken place – a thing without any precedent in History.

125. The most noticeable and important thing is that Gandhiji never cared for the opinion of the people so far as Muslims were concerned. His theme of non-violence had now been deeply soaked in human blood and it was impossible for people to entertain any idea in favor of Pakistan. So long as there is a theocratic State and Government by the side of Indian Union, the peace and tranquility of the Union shall ever remain in danger. But in spite of all these facts, Gandhiji had taken in his hand the task of a propaganda which even the staunchest adherent of the Muslim League would scarcely have been able to do for stopping the spread of unfavorable opinion about Pakistan in the minds of the people.

126. About this very time he resorted to his last fast unto death. Every condition given by him for giving up the fast is in favor of Muslims and against the Hindus.

127. One of the seven conditions imposed by Gandhiji for the breaking of his fast unto death is related to the mosques in Delhi occupied by the Refugees. This condition was to the effect that all the mosques in Delhi which were occupied by the Refugees should be vacated or got vacated and be made over to the Muslims. Gandhiji got this condition accepted by the Government and a number of leaders by sheer coercion brought to bear upon them by his fast. On that day I happened to be in Delhi and I have personally seen some of the events that have occurred in getting this condition carried out to its full. Those were the days of bitter or extreme cold and on the day Gandhiji broke his fast it was also raining, swing to this unusual weather condition, the pricking atmosphere made even person in well-placed positions shiver. Families after families of refugees who had, come to Delhi for shelter were driven out and while doing so no provision was made for their shelter and stay. One or two families taking with them their children, women-folk and what little belongings they had with them and saying, 'Gandhiji, do give us a place for shelter' even approached and came to Birla House. But was it ever possible for the cries of these poor Hindu people to reach Gandhiji living in the palatial Birla House!

I witnessed with my own eyes this scene which would have melted the heart of even a hardhearted person. But thoughts even deeper than this began to come to my mind. Was it out of fun that the refugees found these mosques to be better than their own houses from which they were ousted? Was not Gandhiji aware of the reasons and circumstances that compelled the refugees to occupy the mosques? No Temple and no Gurudwara existed in the part of the country that has become Pakistan. These refugees had seen with their own eyes, their temples and Gurudwaras being desecrated by filthy use made of them simply for the purpose of insulting the Sikhs and Hindus. The refugees had come – fled to Delhi having had to leave every thing belonging to them and there was no place of shelter for them in Delhi. What wonder there could be if the refugees brought to their minds again and again their own hearths and home in the Punjab and N.W.F. Province while they were either taking shelter at the sides of the streets or under a tree somehow? It was under such circumstances that these refugees had resorted to and occupied the mosques. They were living under the roof in mosques and in doing so were not these mosques being used for the benefit of humanity?

While Gandhiji imposed the condition of evacuating the refugees from the mosques occupied by them, had he also asked the Government and the people concerned, to provide some alternative arrangement for their shelter, before getting the mosques evacuated it would have shown some human touch in his demand. While Gandhiji made a demand for the evacuation of the mosques by the refugees had he also imposed a condition to the effect that the temples in Pakistan should be handed over to the Hindus by the Muslims, or some other similar condition, that would have shown that Gandhiji's teaching of non-violence, his anxiety for Hindu-Muslim Unity and his belief in soul force would have been taken or understood as being impartial, spiritual and non-communal. Gandhiji was shrewd enough to know that while undertaking a fast unto death, had he imposed for its break some condition on the Muslims in Pakistan, there would have been found any Muslim who could have shown some grief if the fast ended in the death of Gandhiji. It was for this reason that he purposely avoided imposing any condition on the Muslims.

It was already in his past experience that Mr. Jinnah was not at all perturbed or influenced by his fast and that the Muslim League hardly attached any value to the 'Inner voice' of Gandhiji.

128. It would not be out of place to state here that the remains, i.e. ashes of Gandhiji were distributed in large towns and many rivers in India and abroad but the said ashes could not be immersed in the Holy Indus passing through the Pakistan in spite of the endeavors of Shri Shree Prakash, the Indian High Commissioner in Pakistan.

129. Let us then take the case of 55 crores. Here feed from the Indian Information dated 2nd February 1948 the following extracts:

(a) Extracts from the speech of the Honorable Sardar Vallabhbhai Patel at the press conference held on 12th January, 1948.

(b) Extract from the speech of the Honorable Sir Shanmukham Chatty.

(c) India's spontaneous gesture of good will, and

(d) An extract from the Honorable Prime Minister's statement.

Gandhiji himself has said about these 55 crores that it is always very difficult to make any Government to alter its decisions. But the Government have altered and changed their original decision of withholding the payment of Rs. 55 crores of Pakistan and the reason for doing so was his fast, unto death. (Gandhiji's sermon at Prayer-Meeting held on or about the 21st of January 1948). The decision to withhold the payment of Rs. 55 cores to Pakistan was taken up by our Government which claims to be the people's Government. But this decision of the people's Government was reversed to suit the tune of Gandhiji's fast. It was evident to my mind that the force of public opinion was nothing but a trifle when compared with the leanings of Gandhiji favorable to Pakistan.

130. The creation of Pakistan is the result of the Muslim hostility to the national movement of India. A number of people who showed their allegiance to Pakistan have been clapped in jail as fifth columnists by this very Government. But to my mind Gandhiji himself was the

greatest supporter and advocate of Pakistan and no power could have any control on hire in this attitude of his.

131. In these circumstances the only effective remedy to relieve the Hindus from the Muslim atrocities was, to my mind, to remove Gandhiji from this world.

132. Gandhiji is being referred to as the Father of the Nation – an epithet of high reverence. But if so, he has failed in his paternal duty in as much as he has acted very treacherously to the nation by his consenting to the partitioning of it. Had Gandhiji really maintained his opposition to the creation of Pakistan the Muslim League could have had no strength to claim it and the Britishers also could not have created it in spite of all their utmost efforts for its establishment. The reason for this is not far to seek. The people of this country were eager and vehement in their opposition to Pakistan. But Gandhiji played false with the people and gave parts of the country to the Muslims for the creation of Pakistan. I stoutly maintain that Gandhiji in doing so has failed in his duty which was incumbent upon him to carry out as the Father of the Nation. He has proved to be the Father of Pakistan.

It was for this reason alone that I as a dutiful son of Mother India thought it my duty to put an end to the life of the so-called Father of the Nation who had played a very prominent part in bringing about the vivisection of the country – Our Motherland.

133. The case of Hyderabad had also the same history. It is not at all necessary to refer to the atrocious misdeeds

perpetrated by the Nizam's Ministers and the Razakars. Laik Ali the Prime Minister of Hyderabad had an interview with Gandhiji during the last week of January 1948. It was evident from the manner in which Gandhiji looked at these Hyderabad affairs that Gandhiji would soon start his experiments of non-violence in the State of Hyderabad and treat Kasim Razvi as his adopted son just as Suhrawardy. It was not at all difficult to see that is was impossible for the Government in spite of all the powers to take any strong measures against the Muslim State like Hyderabad so long as Gandhiji was there. Had the Government then decided to take any military of police action against Hyderabad it would have been compelled to withdraw its decision just as was done in the case of the payment of Rs. 55 crores, for Gandhiji would have gone on fast unto death and Government's hands would have been forced to save the life of Gandhiji.

134. The practice of non-violence according to Gandhiji is to endure or put up with the blows of the aggressor without showing any resistance either by weapon or by physical force. Gandhiji has, while describing his non-violence given the example of a 'tiger becoming a follower of the creed of non-violence after the cows allowed themselves to be killed and swallowed in such large numbers that the tiger ultimately got tired of killing them.' It will be remembered that at Kanpur, Ganesh Shanker Vidyarthi fell a victim to the murderous assault by the Muslims of the place on him. Gandhiji lies often cited this submission to the Muslims' blows as an ideal example of embracing

death for the creed of non-violence. I firmly believed and believe that the non-violence of the type described above will lead the nation to ruin and make it easy for Pakistan to enter the remaining India and occupy the same.

135. Briefly speaking, I thought to myself and foresaw that I shall be totally ruined and the only thing that I could expect from the people would be nothing but hatred and that I shall have lost my entire honor even more valuable than my life, if I were for kill Gandhiji. But at the same time I felt that the Indian politics in the absence of Gandhiji would surely be practical, able to retaliate, and would be powerful with armed forces. No doubt my own future would be totally ruined but the nation would be saved from the inroads of Pakistan. People may even call me and dub me as devoid of any sense or foolish, but the nation would be free to follow the course founded on reason which I consider to be necessary for sound nation building.

After having fully considered the question, I took the final decision in the matter but I did not speak about it to any one whatsoever. I took courage in my both hands and I did fire the shots at Gandhiji on 30th January, 1948 on the prayer grounds in Birla House.

136. There now remains hardly anything for me to say. If devotion to one's country amounts to a sin, I admit I have committed that sin, if it is meritorious, I humbly claim the merit thereof. I fully and confidently believe that if there be any other court of justice beyond the one founded

by the mortals, my act will not be taken as unjust. If after the death there be no such place to reach or to go, there is nothing to be said. I have resorted to the action I did purely for the benefit of the humanity. I do say that my shots were fired at the person whose policy and action had brought rack and ruin and destruction to lakhs of Hindus.

137. Really speaking, my life also came to an end simultaneously with the shorts fired by me at Gandhiji. Since then I have been passing my days as if in trance and meditation. Whatever I have seen and observed during this time has given me complete satisfaction.

138. The problem of the State of Hyderabad which had been unnecessarily delayed and postponed has been rightly solved by our Government by the use of armed force after the demise of Gandhiji. The present Government of the remaining India is seen taking the course of practical Politics. The Home Member is said to have expressed the view that the nation must be possessed of armies fully equipped with modern arms and fighting machinery. While giving out such expressions he does say that such a step would be in keeping with the ideal of Gandhiji. He may say so for his satisfaction. But one must not forget that if that were so there would be no difference in the means for the protection of the country devised by Hitler, Mussolini or Churchill or Roosevelt, and scheme based on non-violence as envisaged by Gandhiji. It would then

be impossible to say that there was any new and special message of nonviolence of Gandhiji.

139. I am prepared to concede that Gandhiji did undergo sufferings for the sake of the nation. He did bring about an awakening in the minds of the people. He also did nothing for personal gain; but it pains me to say that he was not honest enough to acknowledge the defeat and failure of the principle of non-violence on all sides. I have read the lives of other intelligent and powerful Indian patriots who have made sacrifices even greater than those done by Gandhiji. I have seen personally some of them. But whatever that may be, I shall bow in respect to the service done by Gandhiji to the country, and to Gandhiji himself for the said service, and before I fired the shots I actually wished him and bowed to him in reverence. But I do maintain that even this servant of the country had no right to vivisect the country – the image of our worship – by deceiving the people. But he did it all the same. There was no legal machinery by which such an offender could be brought to book and it was therefore that I resorted to the firing of shots at Gandhiji as that was the only thing for me to do.

140. Had this act not been done by me, of course it would have been better for me. But circumstances were beyond my control. So strong was the impulse of my mind that I felt that this man should not be allowed to meet a natural death so that the world may know that he had to pay the penalty of his life for his unjust, anti-national and

dangerous favoritism towards a fanatical section of the country. I decided to put an end to this matter and to the further massacre of lakhs of Hindus for no fault of theirs. May God now pardon him for his egoistic nature which proved to be too disastrous for the beloved sons of this Holy Land.

141. I bear no ill-will or enmity towards anyone individual. Nor do I think that any person is inimical towards me personally. I do say that I had no respect for the present Government owing to their policy which was unfairly favorable towards the Muslims. But at the same time I could clearly see that the policy was entirely due to the presence of Gandhiji in that behalf. But in the absence of such pressure, the way is now open for the establishment of a secular State in the true sense of that word. I have to say with great regret that the Hon'ble Prime Minister Pandit Nehruji quite forgets that his actions and deeds are at times opposed to each other, when he talks about secular State in season and out of season; because it is significant to note that the Hon'ble Pandit Nehruji has himself taken a leading part in acquiescing to the establishment of Pakistan, a theocratic State. But he should have realized that it will never bring prosperity to Indian Union with a State founded on fantastically blind religious faith and basis by its side. After having considered absolutely to myself, my mind impelled me to take the action against Gandhiji. No one has brought and could bring any pressure on me in this act of mine.

142. The Honorable Court may take any view in regard to the impulse my mind received and the action I did there under and may pass against me such orders of sentence as may be proper. I have no desire to say anything about it. I do not desire any mercy to be shown to me. I do not also wish that anyone on my behalf should beg for mercy towards me.

143. Several persons are arraigned along with me in this trial as conspirators. I have already said that in the act I did, I had no companions and I alone am solely responsible for my act. Had they not been arraigned with me I would not have even given any defense for me as would be clear from the fact that I desired and enjoined upon my counsel not to cross examine any of the witnesses connected with the incident of the 30th of January, 1948.

144. I have already made it clear that personally I had never accepted the idea of peaceful demonstration even on 20th January, 1948 even for effective propaganda. However, I agreed to join this peaceful demonstration in the prayer-meeting of Gandhiji, though with great reluctance. But as luck would have it, I could not take part in it. And when I found that even such demonstration could not be effectively staged for one reason or the other, I became rather disappointed and desperate. Efforts of Mr. Apte and others to secure volunteers made at Bombay, Poona and Gwalior bore no fruit. I could not then see any other way except to take the extreme course.

145. With these thoughts in my mind, while moving through the refugee Camp in Delhi, I met a photographer with a camera on his back. He asked me to get myself photographed. He seemed to be a refugee. I agreed and got myself photographed by him. On returning to the Delhi Railway Station, I wrote two letters to Apte giving a faint idea of my mental state enclosing therewith my photographs as I felt it my duty to inform Mr Nanarao Apte as he was my close associate in my business of the press; one of such letter was addressed to him personally at his home address at Poona and another was sent to the Hindu Rashtra Office.

146. I wish to further state that all the statements made by me herein are entirely true and correct and each of them is made by reference to authoritative reference books I have made use of the several issues of the Indian Information, an official organ of the Government of India for the information of the public, Indian Year Book, History of the Congress, Gandhiji's Autobiography, Congress Bulletins issued from time to time and the files of Harijan and Young India, and Gandhiji's Post Prayer speeches. I have made this rather long statement not because I want the people to eulogize my act. My only object, in doing so is to leave no room for any misunderstanding about me, and there should be no vagueness in their mind about my views.

147. May the country properly known as Hindustan be again united and be one, and may the people be taught to discard the defeatist mentality leading them to submit

to the aggressors. This is my last wish and prayer to the Almighty.

148. I have now finished; but before I sit down must sincerely and respectfully express my gratitude to Your Honor for the patient hearing given, courtesy shown and facilities given to me. Similarly I express my gratitude to my legal advisers and counsel for their legal help in this great trial. I have no ill-will towards the Police Officers concerned with this case. I sincerely thank them for the kindness and the treatment given by them to me. Similarly, I also thank the Jail authorities for the good treatment given by them.

149. It is a fact that in the presence of a crowd numbering 300 to 400 people I did fire shots at Gandhiji in open daylight. I did not make any attempt to run away; in fact I never entertained any idea of running away. I did not try to shoot myself. It was never my intention to do so, for it was my ardent desire to give vent to my thoughts in an open Court.

150. My confidence about the moral side of my action has not been shaken even by the criticism leveled of against it on all sides. I have no doubt honest writers of history will weigh my act and find the true value thereof on some day in future.

'AKHANDA BHARAT AMAR RAHE'

'VANDE MATARAM'
Delhi, 8-11-1948

SUMMARY OF LIST OF DOCUMENTS ANNEXED

(1) Dy. Prime Minister's statement dated January 12, 1948. Payment of Cash Balance to Pakistan. Late Sardar Valabhbhai Patel, then Dy. Prime Minister has in his statement exposed Pakistan's highhandedness and double game of acquiring cash balances from India and at the same time continuing the invasion on Kashmir, he has strongly defended in the statement India's stand on withholding the money.

(2) The Finance Minister's account of negotiations reaffirms Sardar Patel's stand and sounds a note of warning that India cannot be cowed down by the campaign of hectoring, bullying and scandalizing on the part of responsible Ministers of Pakistan.

(3) The extract "India's spontaneous gesture of goodwill" first reiterates India's stand as just but then it yields to Gandhiji's fast and declares immediate release of the cash balances of Rs. 55 crores.

(4) This in an extract from the Prime Minister's statement. It avers that after consultation with Gandhiji Government had decided to release Rs. 55 crores.

(5) The resolutions of Hindu Mahasabha at its Bilaspur session in December, 1944: They were supported by Shri N. V. Godse.

(i) Basic principles of Constitution of independent Hindustan which will be styled as "Constitution of Hindustan Free State."

(ii) Historically, politically, ethnologically and culturally Hindustan is one, whole and indivisible and so she shall remain.

(iii) The Government to be democratic and federal in character.

(iv) The Federal Legislature to be bi-cameral in structure.

(v) Election to be on adult franchise on one man one vote basis. The electorates to be joint with reservation of seats for minorities on population basis.

(vi) Fundamental Rights: All citizens to be equal in and before law. There shall be no law, civil or criminal, substantive or procedural, of a discriminative nature.

(vii) No citizen by reason of his color, caste or creed to be prejudiced in any way in regard to public employment, office or power or honor or exercise of any profession, trade of calling.

(viii) All citizens shall, subject to public order or morality, enjoy freedom of conscience and profession and practice of religion and protection of culture and language and no law shall be made directly or indirectly to endow any religion or prohibit or restrict the free exercise thereof or give any preference or impose disability on account of religious belief of religious status.

THE COURT SCENE

Justice Khosla, after retirement in a pen picture of the Court scene as it then passed before his mind's eye.

The highlight of the appeal before us was the discourse delivered by Nathuram Godse in his defense. He spoke for several hours, discussing, in the first instance, the facts of the case and then the motive which had prompted him to take Mahatma Gandhi's life.

"The audience was visibly and audibly moved. There was a deep silence when he ceased speaking. Many women were in tears and men coughing and searching for their handkerchiefs. The silence was accentuated and made deeper by the sound of an occasional subdued sniff or a muffled cough...

"I have however, no doubt that had the audience of that day been constituted into a jury and entrusted with the task of deciding Godse's appeal, they would have brought in a verdict of 'not guilty' by an overwhelming majority."

Nathuram had displayed the same ability while arguing his case before Shri Atma Charan, the Judge of the Special Court, Red Fort, Delhi.

NATHURAM GODSE'S WILL

The will of Nathuram is in the form of a letter in Hindi, addressed to Shri Dattatraya Vinayak Godse, his younger brother. The Magistrate put a seal over it on November 15, 1949. The Jail authorities passed on the letter to Shri Dattatraya.

Nathuram left behind his only valuable property – his ashes – and instructed how to dispose them of.

The Will

Ambala Jail,

My dear Dattatraya,

You are allowed to perform last rites of my body you may perform them in any manner. But I am to express herewith a specific wish.

The river Indus (Sindhu), on the banks of which our Pre-historic Rishis composed the Vedas is the Boundary of our Bharatvarsha i.e. Hindustan.

My ashes may be sunk in the Holy Sindhu river when she will again flow freely under the aegis of the flag of Hindustan. That will be the sacred day for us.

It hardly matters even if it took a couple of generations for realizing my wish. Preserve the ashes till then, and if that day would not dawn in your life time, pass on the remains to posterity for translating my desire into reality.

If and when the Government lifts ban on my statement made in the Court, I authorize you to publish it.

14-11-1949

Nathuram Vinayak Godse

I have donated Rs. 101/- on this day for its utilization for the dome (kalasha) of the sacred Somnath temple which is under construction.

15-11-1949
Nathuram Vinayak Godse